HIMACHAL PRADESH

A STATE STUDY GUIDE

HARISH SINGH RATHORE

Published by

Hawk Press
4836/24, Ansari Road, Daryaganj
New Delhi – 110 002
Phones: 91-11-23278618, 91-11-43667199
E-mail: thehawkpress@gmail.com
www.thehawkpress.com

ISBN: 978-93-88318-85-3

Preface

Himachal Pradesh is a state in northern part of India. Situated in the Western Himalayas, it is bordered by states of Jammu and Kashmir on the north, Punjab on the west, Haryana on the southwest, Uttarakhand on the southeast, and Tibet on the east. At its southernmost point, it also touches the state of Uttar Pradesh. The state's name was coined from the Sanskrit—Him means 'snow' and achal means 'land' or 'abode'—by acharya Diwakar Datt Sharma, one of the state's eminent Sanskrit scholars.

The state is spread across valleys. About 90% of the state's population lives in rural areas. Many perennial rivers flow in the state with numerous hydropower plants producing surplus electricity that is sold to other states, such as Delhi, Punjab and West Bengal. Tourism and agriculture are also important constituents of the state's economy. The state has one of the highest per-capita incomes among the Indian states and union territories.

The villages have good connectivity with roads and public health centres. Practically all houses have a toilet and 100% hygiene has been achieved in the state. Notable actions by the state government include a ban on polyethylene bags and tobaccoproducts. According to a survey of CMS - India Corruption Study 2017, Himachal Pradesh is India's least corrupt state.

The Government of Himachal Pradesh also known as the State Government of Himachal Pradesh, or locally as State Government, is the supreme governing authority of the Indian state of Himachal Pradesh. It consists of an executive branch, led by the Governor of Himachal Pradesh, a judiciary and a legislative branch.

Himachal is one of those states in India which was rapidly transformed from the most backward part of the country to one of the most advanced states. At present Himachal ranks fourth in respect of per capita income among the states of the Indian Union.

Himachal education system is well established, its agriculture is enough for its self-sufficiency, its horticulture is highly impressive in the country and even in abroad, its road connectivity system has emerged as the best in the mountainous areas in India, the infrastructure for its industrial development are well laid out, its rich forest resources being augmented and above all, the increasing attention of the nation towards the exploitation of its hydel resources are the signs for its bright future. It has already become the ideal in respect of development for the hill areas of the country.

Tourism in Himachal Pradesh relates to tourism in the Indian state of Himachal Pradesh. Himachal Pradesh is famous for its Himalayan landscapes and popular hill-stations. Many outdoor activities such as rock climbing, mountain biking, paragliding, ice-skating, and heli-skiing are popular tourist attractions in Himachal Pradesh.

This is a reference book. All the matter is just compiled and edited in nature, taken from the various sources which are in public domain.

This is the first comprehensive volume to appear on the Art and Architecture of Himachal Pradesh, and it includes sections on Hindu and Buddhist Architecture in the Western Himalaya Sculpture bronzes, woodcarving Pahari painting and Chamba Rumals. It contains also an extensive and invaluable bibliography and an equally invaluable list of temples the most complete so far undertaken the author having obtained the name location and style of each shrine from the relevant district officers stationed throughout the state. The book enlightens and refreshes the readers by providing an insight into this wonderful state.

—Editor

ABOUT THE BOOK

Himachal Pradesh is a state in northern part of India. Situated in the Western Himalayas, it is bordered by states of Jammu and Kashmir on the north, Punjab on the west, Haryana on the southwest, Uttarakhand on the southeast, and Tibet on the east. At its southernmost point, it also touches the state of Uttar Pradesh. The state's name was coined from the Sanskrit—Him means 'snow' and achal means 'land' or 'abode'—by acharya Diwakar Datt Sharma, one of the state's eminent Sanskrit scholars. Himachal is a mosaic of different cultures. It is inhabited by one of the most colourful people whose culture is as richly diverse and fascinating as the landscape. The developmental activities such as industrialization, road construction, hydropower projects, horticulture, urbanization, mining and growth of tourism have gradually transformed the state, though the issues of environmental pollution, resource depletion and increasing incidences of natural hazards such as cloudbursts, flash floods, land-slides and erratic weather conditions are causing serious concerns. This is the first comprehensive volume to appear on the Art and Architecture of Himachal Pradesh, and it includes sections on Hindu and Buddhist Architecture in the Western Himalaya Sculpture bronzes, woodcarving Pahari painting and Chamba Rumals. It contains also an extensive and invaluable bibliography and an equally invaluable list of temples the most complete so far undertaken the author having obtained the name location and style of each shrine from the relevant district officers stationed throughout the state. The book enlightens and refreshes the readers by providing an insight into this wonderful state.

Contents

1

State at a Glance

Himachal Pradesh is a state in northern part of India. Situated in the Western Himalayas, it is bordered by states of Jammu and Kashmir on the north, Punjab on the west, Haryana on the southwest, Uttarakhand on the southeast, and Tibet on the east. At its southernmost point, it also touches the state of Uttar Pradesh. The state's name was coined from the Sanskrit—*Him* means 'snow' and *achal* means 'land' or 'abode'—by acharya Diwakar Datt Sharma, one of the state's eminent Sanskrit scholars.

The state is spread across valleys. About 90% of the state's population lives in rural areas. Many perennial rivers flow in the state with numerous hydropower plants producing surplus electricity that is sold to other states, such as Delhi, Punjab and West Bengal. Tourism and agriculture are also important constituents of the state's economy. The state has one of the highest per-capita incomes among the Indian states and union territories.

The villages have good connectivity with roads and public health centres. Practically all houses have a toilet and 100% hygiene has been achieved in the state. Notable actions by the state government include a ban on polyethylene bags and tobaccoproducts. According to a survey of CMS - India Corruption Study 2017, Himachal Pradesh is India's least corrupt state.

STATE PROFILE

Kalpa, a typical town in Himachal Pradesh

Sunrise in Himachal Pradesh, at Kinnaur Kailash

Sunshine on a snowy mountain at Himachal Pradesh

Snowy mountain range appears to be in sky

Source: *Department of Information and Public Relations.*

Area	**55,673 km²**
Total population	6,864,602
Males	3,481,873
Females	3,382,729
Population density	123
Sex ratio	972
Rural population	6,176,050
Urban population	688,552
Scheduled Caste population	1,729,252
Scheduled Tribe population	392,126
Literacy rate	83.78%
Male literacy	90.83%
Female literacy	76.60%
Capitals	2

Districts	12
Sub-divisions	62
Tehsils	149
Sub-tehsils	35
Developmental blocks	78
Towns	59
Panchayats	3,226
Panchayat smities	77
Zila parishad	12
Urban local bodies	49
Nagar nigams	2
Nagar parishads	25
Nagar panchayats	23
Census villages	20,690
Inhabited villages	17,495
Health institutions	3,866
Educational institutions	17,000
Motorable roads	33,722 km
National highways	8
Identified hydroelectric potential	23,000.43 MW in five rivers basins i.e. (Yamuna, Satluj, Beas, Ravi, Chenab and Himurja)
Potential harnessed	10,264 MW
Food grain production	1579,000 tonnes
Vegetable production	900,000 tonnes
Fruit production	1,027,000 tonnes
Per capita income	158,462 (2017–18)
Social Security pensions	237,250 persons, annual expenditure: over 600 million
Investment in industrial areas	273.80 billion, employment opportunities: Over 337,391
Employment generated in government sector	80,000

Census 2011- Largest District (km^2) (1) Lahul and Spiti 13841 (2) Chamba 6522 (3) Kinnaur 6401 (4) Kangra 5739 (5) Kullu 5503

Highest Percentage of Child Population (1) Chamba 13.55% (2) Sirmaur 13.14% (3) Solan 11.74% (4) Kullu 11.52% (5) Una 11.36%

Highest Density (1) Hamirpur 407 (2) Una 338 (3) Bilaspur 327 (4) Solan 300 (5) Kangra 263

Top Population Growth (1) Una 16.26% (2) Solan 15.93% (3) Sirmaur 15.54% (4) Kullu 14.76% (5) Kangra 12.77%

Highest Literacy (1) Hamirpur 100% (2) Una 87.23% (3) Kangra 86.49% (4) Blaspur 85.87% (5) Solan 85.02%

Highest Sex Ratio (1) Hamirpur 1050 (2) Kangra 1012 (3) Mandi 1007 (4) Chamba 986 (5) Bilaspur 981

HISTORY OF HIMACHAL PRADESH

Himachal Pradesh was established in 1948 as a Chief Commissioner's Province within the Union of India. The Himachal History The province comprised the hill districts around Shimla and southern hill areas of the former Punjab region. Himachal became a part C state on 26 January 1950 with the implementation of the Constitution of India. Himachal Pradesh became a Union Territory on 1 November 1956. On 18 December 1970 the State of Himachal Pradesh Act was passed by Parliament and the new state came into being on 25 January 1971. Thus Himachal emerged as the eighteenth state of the Indian Union.

In earlier times, the area was variously divided among smaller kingdoms, such as those of Chamba, Bilaspur, Bhagal and Dhami. After the Gurkha War of 1815–1816, it became part of the British India.

Pre-Independence

The history of the area that now constitutes Himachal Pradesh dates to the Indus valley civilisation that flourished between 2250 and 1750 BCE. Tribes such as the Koli, Hali,

Dagi, Dhaugri, Dasa, Khasa, Kinnar, and Kirat inhabited the region from the prehistoric era.

During the Vedic period, several small republics known as *Janapada* existed which were later conquered by the Gupta Empire. After a brief period of supremacy by King Harshavardhana, the region was divided into several local powers headed by chieftains, including some Rajput principalities.

These kingdoms enjoyed a large degree of independence and were invaded by Delhi Sultanatea number of times. Mahmud Ghaznavi conquered Kangra at the beginning of the 10th century. Timur and Sikander Lodi also marched through the lower hills of the state and captured a number of forts and fought many battles. Several hill states acknowledged Mughal suzerainty and paid regular tribute to the Mughals.

The Kingdom of Gorkha conquered many kingdoms and came to power in Nepal in 1768.They consolidated their military power and began to expand their territory. Gradually, the Kingdom of Nepal annexed Sirmour and Shimla. Under the leadership of Amar Singh Thapa, the Nepali army laid siege to Kangra.

They managed to defeat Sansar ChandKatoch, the ruler of Kangra, in 1806 with the help of many provincial chiefs. However, the Nepali army could not capture Kangra fort which came under Maharaja Ranjeet Singh in 1809. After the defeat, they began to expand towards the south of the state. However, Raja Ram Singh, Raja of Siba State, captured the fort of Siba from the remnants of Lahore Darbar in Samvat 1846, during the First Anglo-Sikh War.

They came into direct conflict with the British along the *tarai* belt after which the British expelled them from the provinces of the Satluj. The British gradually emerged as the paramount power in the region. In the revolt of 1857, or first Indian war of independence, arising from a number of grievances against the British, the people of the hill states were not as politically active as were those in other parts of the country.

They and their rulers, with the exception of Bushahr, remained more or less inactive. Some, including the rulers of Chamba, Bilaspur, Bhagal and Dhami, rendered help to the British government during the revolt.

Rock Cut Temple, Masroor

The British territories came under the British Crown after Queen Victoria's proclamation of 1858. The states of Chamba, Mandi and Bilaspur made good progress in many fields during the British rule.

During World War I, virtually all rulers of the hill states remained loyal and contributed to the British war effort, both in the form of men and materials. Among these were the states of Kangra, Jaswan, Datarpur, Guler, Rajgarh, Nurpur, Chamba, Suket, Mandi, and Bilaspur.

After independence, the Chief Commissioner's Province of Himachal Pradesh was organized on 15 April 1948 as a result of integration of 28 petty princely states (including feudal princes and *zaildars*) in the promontories of the western Himalayas. These were known as the Simla Hills States and four Punjab southern hill states under the Himachal Pradesh (Administration) Order, 1948 under Sections 3 and 4 of the Extra-Provincial Jurisdiction Act, 1947 (later renamed as the Foreign Jurisdiction Act, 1947 vide A.O. of 1950). The State of Bilaspur was merged into Himachal Pradesh on 1 July 1954 by the Himachal Pradesh and Bilaspur (New State) Act, 1954.

Himachal became a Part 'C' state on 26 January 1950 with the implementation of the Constitution of India and the Lieutenant Governor was appointed. The Legislative Assembly was elected in 1952. Himachal Pradesh became a union territory on 1 November 1956. Some areas of Punjab State— namely Simla, Kangra, Kullu and Lahul and Spiti Districts, Nalagarh tehsil of Ambala District, Lohara, Amb and Una kanungo circles, some area of Santokhgarh kanungo circle and some other specified area of Una tehsil of Hoshiarpur District, besides some parts of Dhar Kalan Kanungo circle of Pathankot tehsil of Gurdaspur District—were merged with Himachal Pradesh on 1 November 1966 on enactment by Parliament of Punjab Reorganisation Act, 1966. On 18 December 1970, the State of Himachal Pradesh Act was passed by Parliament, and the new state came into being on 25 January 1971. Himachal became the 18th state of the Indian Union with Dr. Yashwant Singh Parmar as its first chief minister.

Prehistory

Some evidences have been found that nearly 2 million years ago man lived in the foothills of Himachal Pradesh. Bangana valley of Kangra, *Sirsa* valley of Nalagarhand *Markanda* valley of Sirmour are found to be the places where prehistoric man used to live. The foothills of the state were inhabited by people from Indus valley civilization which flourished between the time period of 2250 and 1750 BC. Before indus valley civilization koli, holi, dooms and chnnals are used to live here. The famous war between the Aryan King Devodas and Kirat's King Shambhar found mention in the Rigveda. King Shambhar had 99 forts in mid Himalayan region of modern Himachal.He had to loose the war which lasted 40 years.

Medieval history

In about 883 AD Shankar Verma, the ruler of Kashmir exercised his influence over Himachal Pradesh. The region also witnessed the invasion of Mahmud Ghazni in 1009 AD, who during that period looted the wealth from the temples in the North India. In 1043 AD the Rajputs ruled over the territory.

In 1773 AD the Rajputs under Katoch Maharaja Sansar Chand-II possessed the region, until the attack by Maharaja Ranjit Singh in 1804 which crushed the Rajput power.

The small kingdom enjoyed a large degree of independence till the eve of the Muslim invasions in northern India. The states of the foothills were devastated by Muslim invaders a number of times. Mahmud Ghaznavi conquered Kangra at the beginning of the 10th century. Timur and Sikander Lodi also marched through the lower hills of the state and captured a number of forts and fought many battles.

The *Gorkhas*, a martial tribe came to power in Nepal in 1768. They consolidated their military power and began to expand their territory.

The Gurkhas marched in from Nepal and captured the area. Gradually the Gorkhas annexed Sirmour and Shimla. Under the leadership of Bada Kaji (equivalent to General) Amar Singh Thapa, *Gorkhas* laid siege to Kangra. They managed to defeat Sansar Chand, the ruler of Kangra, in 1806. However *Gorkhas* could not capture Kangra fort which came under Maharaja Ranjit Singh in 1809.

British period

This led to the *Anglo-Gorkha* war. They came into direct conflict with the British along the *tarai* belt after which the British expelled them from the provinces of the Satluj. Thus British gradually emerged as the paramount powers. In early 19th century the British annexed the areas of Shimla after the Gurkha War of 1815–16. Himachal became a centrally administered territory in 1948 with the integration of 31 hill provinces and received additional regions in 1966.

The revolt of 1857 or the first Indian war of independence resulted due to the building up of political, social, economic, religious and military grievances against the British government. People of the hill states were not politically alive as the people in other parts of the country. They remained more or less inactive and so did their rulers with the exception of *Bushahr*.

Some of them even rendered help to the British government during the revolt. Among them were the rulers of Chamba, Bilaspur, Bhagal and Dhami. The rulers of Bushars rather acted in a manner hostile to the interests of British.

The British territories in the hill came under British Crown after Queen Victoria's proclamation of 1858. The states of Chamba, Mandi and Bilaspur made good progress in many fields during the British rule. During World War I, virtually all rulers of the hill states remained loyal and contributed to the British war effort both in the form of men and materials. Amongst these were the states of Kangra, Nurpur, Chamba, Suket, Mandi and Bilaspur.

Post independence

After independence the *Chief Commissioner's province of H.P.* came into being on 15 April 1948. Himachal became a part C state on Sept. 1951 with the implementation of the Constitution of India. Himachal Pradesh became Union Territory on 1 November 1956. On 18 December 1970 the State of Himachal Pradesh Act was passed by Parliament and the new state came into being on 25 January 1971. Thus H.P. emerged as the eighteenth state of Indian Union.

Under the name of Greater Nepal, some in Nepal have asked for the return of states previously usurped by Nepal that were annexed by the British East India Company. However, little support for this motion exists in these regions.

LAWS

Crime and Punishment: People in Himachal are simple and peace loving. Stealing, killing or taking away some one else's share is considered sinful. Long litigations are sometimes caused due to land or women related problems. Among the lower castes abducting someone's wife or the wife's elopement causes minor scuffles but none of them are very serious. People here forgive easily. The women are more prone to suicide as the social pressures are more intense on them.

The quarrels within a caste or community are usually decided by Doom or Khumli (the community panchayat). The local priest and Kardar (head) are members of this. The Kardar signifies the date and the priest calls the assembly. An emergency meeting is known as Thek, Dadhi or Dal in which each absentee has to pay a fine of a rupee. In some areas of Kulu, Kinnaur and Mahasu, the gods are called upon to decide matters. In Malana, the god Jamlu and the god Mahasu in Dodra Kwar decide the cases through their devotees. Their judgment are final and irrevocable.

People who defy the caste laws are ostracised. This custom is known as Chekka or Banaj. A family which has been ostracised is not visited by the fellow villagers. Such people or families can be accepted back into the community only if the whole community assembles in the village and agrees to call the defaulter. He is then made to drink the holy Panch Gava (a holy mixture of five products of the holy cow comprising of her milk, butter, ghee, urine and dung) and then he may sit with the members of his community at a feast. After this he offers a gift to the god. The local king is also given a gift (shojir) of money.

Killing a cow is considered the biggest crime and sin. A man who commits it, is debarred from the village till he goes to holy places like Mattan or Haridwar and has a Havan performed at his house. People trust each other and often leave their property and animals in each other's care without any formal written documents. To dig into someone else's savings is considered highly sinful. Charging an interest on a loan, selling milk or charging a rent for lodging someone in one's house are all looked down upon. These customs are undergoing changes now.

The village money lender usually takes advantage of the illiteracy of the villagers by charging them exorbitant interest rates. Some of such loans can never be paid in full. The system of opening banks in villages by the government has improved the situation.

Now each village has a Panchayat and most of the reforms and litigations are affected by these. People cast votes to choose the members of this assembly. Fallow land around the village is known as Shamlat. This is a common property and can be used as grazing land for cattle. The village fairs, festivals and folk-plays take place here.

Hereditary Laws: The laws of heredity differ from area to area. The hereditary rights pass direct from the father to the son or sons. In case of there being more than one wife, children of all the wives may claim an equal share. If some one has no son, his property is shared equally by the daughters. If the daughter dies issueless, the property then passes on to the father's relatives.

In Spiti the customs are a little different. There the family system is called Jethansi. As the eldest son gets married, he shall become the head of the house and the father shall retire to a smaller house.

The eldest son then comes to be known as Rambagchepa and the retired father as Ravangechugpa. The father gets a small plot of land to live by and the younger sons join a monastery.

In case the eldest son produces no male heirs, the younger brother may become the head and shoulder the family responsibilities. The land in the area is thus prevented from getting sub divided.

In case none of the sons produces a son, the daughter of the house is then married to a man who agrees to come and live in his father-in-law's house and carry on the family traditions. Such a son-in-law is known as Makpa. If the girl dies, or does not have children, the husband may then marry a cousin of hers who then stands to inherit the property.

In Kinnaur and Mahasu many families follow the system of polyandry. In such families when the husband dies, the wife as also property, passes to the next brother and after him the right of property then reverts back to the sons. Illegitimate children or children born of a widow or an unmarried girl have no property rights.

They are known as Poltu or Chukandu. Earlier they were used by families as domestic servants and in exchange for their services a small plot of land was given to them. Now they have legal protection against such exploitation and if they can establish their paternity, they can inherit a share of the paternal property.

Some areas follow the customs of Jethand, Paghand and Chundband. In Jethand the eldest son inherits a larger share of the property plus a larger share of his family debts. In Chundaband system all the sons of the various wives have equal share in the paternal property. In Paghand system the property shall first be distributed among the daughter and then among the sons.

This custom is prevalent among the Gaddis. Among the Rajputs there existed a system known as Daya Bhag (the rightful position). In this, the eldest son stands to inherit a special portion in addition to his other share by virtue of being the eldest son.

SOCIOECONOMIC STRUCTURES

Most of the people in the state are farmers or farm labourers and live in the villages. These people are a close knit community and are ever willing to co-operate with their fellow villagers and share their problems. Most people earn their living through farming. The hill tribes also rear goats, sheep, horses and mules. Some tribes earn their living by grazing cattle, crushing stones or searching for and collecting medicinal herbs.

The villages follow a neat and orderly pattern. Each village has people, belonging to different castes and income groups. The carpenters, the barbers, the ironsmiths and the Kahars help the landowners with petty form jobs or other necessary work. They are paid in kind and not in cash. These tribes also help each other in following the rituals and customs at the time of a death or a birth.

The larger farms lie outside the villages and are owned by a few rich landlords. People belonging to the lower castes also do begar (work with no payment) for the landlord. The new land reforms and legislations have changed the situation to a certain extent.

The villages follow a Panchayat system. The Panchayat is responsible for development work within the village. The people worship the land and it is supposed to be sinful to steal or sell it. The land is the farmer's sole, property, although at times he is forced to pawn it. The fallow land within or outside the village is known as shamlat. It is considered as communal property.

The settlement follows the caste pattern. The settlements of the higher caste Brahmins, the Rajputs, the Mahajans (money lenders) are beautifully kept and well looked after. The Rajput live close to the hills and forests. They follow the purdah system. The moneylenders and the Khatris live to the cities. The Brahmins live both in the rural and the urban areas. The houses of the lower caste are usually on the outskirts of the villages. The smiths have their foundries inside the house where they work morning and evening.

The villages attach a great importance to brotherhood. When arranging wedding-matches, the caste and Gotra is given importance. People prefer to marry into families with similar backgrounds both religious and economic and into neighbouring villages so that kinship may grow. Each caste is keen to retain its traditions and values. The lower castes are now aware of the benefits of working and living as a community. The joint family system is encouraged and the familiar relationships are cherished and filial devotion is given high priority. The sister is highly respected and other relationships are also given due importance.

The houses are built of clay bricks and the roofs are of slate. In the hill areas stones are used instead of bricks and timber is used for the roofs. The cattle houses are close to the house. People prefer pucca houses.

The tribals live in double storeyed houses where the ground floor is used for the cattle and the first floor is used as their living quarters. The labourers live in thatched huts. The architectural patterns change from area to area. Among the gods both Aryan and non-Aryan gods are worshipped. Shiva is the chief god among the Gaddis. Vishnu, Krishna and Buddha are also worshipped. There is very little impact of Jainism. The Buddhist Lama religion has had a great impact in the Lahaul, Spiti, Pangi and Kinnaur areas.

2

Culture and Society

CULTURE OF HIMACHAL PRADESH

Himachal Pradesh, the North Indian state, was one of the few states that had remained largely untouched by external customs, largely due to its difficult terrain. With the technological advancements, the state has changed very rapidly. Himachal Pradesh is a multireligional, multicultural as well as multilingual state like other Indian states. Some of the most commonly spoken languages are Hindi and the various Pahari languages. The Hindu communities residing in Himachal include the *Brahmins*, *Rajputs*, *Kannets*, *Rathis* and *Kolis*. There are also tribal population in the state which mainly comprise Gaddis, *Kinnarms*, Gujjars, *Pangawals* and *Lahaulis*.

Himachal is well known for its handicrafts. The carpets, leather works, shawls, paintings, metalware, woodwork and paintings are worth appreciating. Pashmina shawl is one of the products which is highly in demand not only in Himachal but all over the country. Himachali caps are also famous art work of the people.

Local music and dance reflects the cultural identity of the state. Through their dance and music, they entreat their gods during local festivals and other special occasions.

Apart from the fairs and festivals that are celebrated all over India, there are number of other fairs and festivals, including the temple fairs in nearly every region that are of great significance to Himachal Pradesh.

The day to day food of *Himachalis* is very similar to the rest of the north India. They too have lentil, broth, rice, vegetables and bread. As compared to other states in north India non-vegetarian cuisine is more preferred. Some of the specialities of Himachal include *Manee,Madeera,Pateer*, *Chouck*, *Bhagjery* and *chutney* of Til.

Traditional home, Manali

Himachal Pradesh was one of the few states that had remained largely untouched by external customs, largely due to its difficult terrain. With remarkable economic and social advancements, the state has changed very rapidly. Himachal Pradesh is a multireligious, multicultural as well as a multilingual state like other Indian states. Western Pahari languages also known as Himachali languages are widely spoken in the state. Some of the most commonly spoken individual languages are Kangri, Mandeali, Kulvi, Chambeali, Bharmauri and Kinnauri. The Hinducommunities residing in Himachal include the *Brahmins*,

Rajputs, *Kayasthas*, *Sunars*, *Kannets*, *Rathis* and *Kolis*. The tribal population of the state consists mainly of *Gaddis*, *Gujjars*, *Kanauras*, *Pangwalas*, *Bhots*, *Swanglas* and *Lahaulas*.

Nako Village

Himachal is well known for its handicrafts. The carpets, leather works, Kullu shawls, Kangra paintings, Chamba Rumals, stoles, embroidered grass footwear (*Pullan chappal*), silver jewelry, metal-ware, knitted woolen socks, *Pattoo*, basketry of cane and bamboo (*Wicker* and *Rattan*) and woodwork are among the notable ones. Of late, the demand for these handicrafts has increased within and outside the country.Himachali caps of various colour bands are also well-known art work of the local people, and are often treated as a symbol of the Himachali identity. The colour of the Himachali caps has been an indicator of political loyalties in the hill state for a long period of time with Congress party leaders like Virbhadra Singh always donning caps with green band and the rival BJP leader Prem Kumar Dhumal always wearing a cap with maroon band. The former has served six terms as the Chief

Minister of the state while the latter is a two-time Chief Minister.Local music and dance also reflects the cultural identity of the state. Through their dance and music, the Himachali people entreat their gods during local festivals and other special occasions.

Apart from the fairs and festivals that are celebrated all over India, there are number of other fairs and festivals, including the temple fairs in nearly every region that are of great significance to Himachal Pradesh. The Kullu Dussehra festival is very famous all over India. The day to day cuisine of *Himachalis* is very similar to the rest of the north India with a significant influence of Punjabi and Tibetan cuisines.Lentils (*Dâl*), rice (*Châwal*), vegetables (*Sabzî*) and chapati (wheat flatbread) form the staple food of the local population. As compared to other states in north India, non-vegetarian food is more preferred and accepted in Himachal Pradesh, partly owing to difficulty in finding a variety of fresh vegetables on the hilly terrain of the state. Some of the local specialities of Himachali cuisine include *Siddu, Babru, Khatta, Mhanee, Channa Madra, Patrode, Mah Ki Dal, Chamba Style Fried Fish, Kullu Trout, Chha Gosht, Pahadi Chicken, Sepu Badi, Auriya Kaddu, Aloo Palda, Pateer, Makki Ki Roti and Sarson Ka Saag, Chouck, Bhagjery* and *Chutney* of Til.

Notable people

- 14th Dalai Lama, Tenzin Gyatso, Nobel Peace Prize recipient and former Head of the Tibetan Government-in-Exile
- Dev Anand, Bollywood actor who studied here
- Shahid Javed Burki, economist and former vice-president of World Bank
- Mohit Chauhan, Bollywood singer
- Siddharth Chauhan, independent filmmaker
- Prem Chopra
- Rubina Dilaik, television actress

- Namrata Singh Gujral, American actress
- Yami Gautam, Bollywood actress
- Allan Octavian Hume, ornithologist
- Hamid Karzai, president of Afghanistan who studied here

Kalachakra Temple in the main street of Mcleod Ganj

- The Great Khali, professional wrestler
- Anupam Kher, Bollywood actor
- Major Som Nath Sharma, the first recipient of the Param Vir Chakra from the state
- Naib Subedar Sanjay Kumar, an Indian Army Junior Commissioned Officer and recipient of the Param Vir Chakra
- Captain Vikram Batra, recipient of the Param Vir Chakra
- Ram Kumar, abstract artist
- Shanta Kumar, member of Lok Sabha
- Vijay Kumar, silver medallist in 25m shooting at the 2012 Summer Olympics
- Mehr Chand Mahajan, Third Supreme Court Chief-Justice and former chief Minister of Kashmir in 1947,
- Jagat Prakash Nadda, member of Lok Sabha and Health Minister of India
- Shyam Saran Negi, named as the first voter of independent India
- Shivya Pathania, television actress
- Karnail Rana, Himachali Folk Singer
- Purva Rana, Miss Femina 2012
- Kangana Ranaut, Bollywood actress
- Idries Shah writer, Sufi teacher and sage
- Anand Sharma, member of Rajya Sabha and former Union Cabinet Minister for Commerce and Industry of the Government of India
- Anuj Sharma, Bollywood singer
- Shriya Sharma, film actress
- Pritam Singh, brand ambassador of the state
- Sobha Singh, painter
- Asmita Sood, television actress
- Satyananda Stokes, who introduced apples to the region
- Ajay Thakur, gold medallist at the Asian Games and World Cup in 2016

- Anurag Thakur, member of Lok Sabha and former President of the Board of Control for Cricket in India
- Muhammad Zia-ul-Haq, former general of Pakistan who studied here
- Preity Zinta, Bollywood actress
- Shiva Keshavan, Winter Olympian
- Adarsh Rathore, Journalist and musician
- Ram Swaroop Sharma, Politician
- Charlie Chauhan, television actress.

CUSTOMS AND TRADITIONS

Tribal and non-tribal communities live together all over Himachal Pradesh. The villages follow their own hierarchies of caste and community patterns, which follow the demands of a life style followed through the ages.

The village is looked upon as a large family. People have established close familiar relationship with each other and address the elder as Chacha-Tau (uncle), Bhabhi (sister-in-law), Mausi (aunt) or Nani (grandmother) according to their ages. The relationship between the wife and the husband's younger brother (Bhabi-Devar) carries a special romanticised aura. Each bride addresses men younger than her husband, as Devar. An elder is addressed as Jija, a women about the same age as one's mother as Mausi and a man younger than one's father as Chacha. All old women in the mother's village are addressed as Nanis and ones in one's own village a Dadi. People close in age address each other as Bhau (male) or Bhain (female). These relationships are looked upon as precious among individuals and in the community.

In the tribal areas also there is a common practice. A women may choose a man as her brother and then they are known as Mitra and Mitrani. At the time of a marriage, the untying of the thread Kankan and at the time of the Karva Chauth fast, the exchange of karwa (clay pots with a snout) are also occasions for making a brother or a sister. The families always treat these relationships with respect.

The mother's brother (Mama) plays an important role at the time of wedding or other family festivities. He presents his sister and her family with gifts of sweets and clothes when the sister has a baby and also when the sacred thread ceremony (Yagyopavit) is performed for her sons. At the time of the sister's wedding, it is the brother who supports her and puts her in palanquin. Most brothers perform their traditional duties towards their sister with affection and respect.

The sister as Nanad or sister-in-law plays an important role in her father's family. The older brother is known as Jeth and his wife as Jithani. These two come next in important to the parents. The parents enjoy the highest place in the family hierarchy and if the son and his wife live in their own houses separately while the parents are alive, it is frowned upon. The older uncles are also highly respected and at the time of a wedding, they are honoured with gifts of pink turbans. Aunts, uncles, cousins are all considered equal to one's own parents and brothers and sisters are loved and respected.

The Rajputs and the Brahmins lay particular stress on the purity of race, caste, gotra and family. Among the higher castes the daughters father's house (Maika) enjoys a great importance. At the time of festivals and major family occasions like a wedding or a birth, various gifts including foodstuffs, jewellery and clothes are sent to the girls husband's house (sasural). It is also taboo for the girl's family members to eat or drink anything in her sasural. They must pay an equivalent sum of money as compensation. Among the lower castes such taboos are not enforced strictly. The higher castes follow a custom of Purdah. Women veil their faces in front of all elders with the head bared. When a girl comes out of her quarters after delivering a child, she must touch the feet of all the elders in her husband's family and leave some money at their feet. This customs is known as Pair Bandai (worshipping the feet).

Marriages are settled at an early age. There are instances of matches being settled between families before the babies are born, based on assumptions that one will be a boy and other a girl.

The relationship between a brother-in-law and a sister-in-law is an informal and a close one. It is customary for the young brother-in-law to be seated in the bride's lap and to be the first to see her face. Among the tribals it is permissible for the younger brother to marry the older brothers widow but the higher castes do not permit this. Among them the older brothers wife is equal to one's mother.

All the brothers and their wives must live with the parents when they are alive. The older brother is considered equal to the father. The polyandrous customs of Kinnaur region also point at the close bond between the brothers.

The occasion of a girl child's birth is not celebrated with great joy. Girls are respected as De (short for Devi or goddess). At the time of the Navratra, special Puja is offered to the young girls and at the time of festivals she is given special gifts of clothing and sweets.

Marriages: Marriage is an important ceremony in Himachal. The parents are also the closer elders relatives begin to look around for suitable matches as soon as the child is old enough. Sometimes a middleman is used as a match-maker known as Roovary, Dhamu or Mazomi. He finds out the details about the social and financial standing of the family and the final decision is taken on the basis of the horoscopes. Matches in the same Gotra are not considered very good. When the match is settled the ritual gift called Tika is sent. The groom and his family are invited to tea. On this occasion ritual songs are sung and sweets are distributed. In the tribal areas both the parties exchange Chhang (rice wine) and close relatives are invited to participate in the ceremony. In some areas during the various festivals, gifts of jewellery and clothes are sent to the betrothed. In Kinnaur this system is known as Chharmi Nata, elsewhere it is known as sending the Tihar.

The date for the wedding is set in consultation with the priest. In some places the permission of the deities is also sought. Customarily all the preparations for the wedding are to be kept a secret from the bride. In Kinnaur as the wedding party approaches the house, the bride and her friends begin to wail and weep.

Marriage customs differ from place to place in Himachal. The bride and the groom are carried in palanquins except in the Lahaul area. The girl touches her father's feet at the time of her departure. People in Kinnaur follow a matriarchal system where all the brothers share a wife and if there are more than six brothers then another may be brought in. All the brothers are looked upon as common fathers to the children. The eldest is known as Teg Bawal and the youngest as Gota Bawal.

A maid (barber's wife or Pachekan) accompanies the bride temporarily from her father's house to help her settle down in the midst of her new family. In Lahaul when the groom departs with the bride the girl friends of the bride block his path till the groom promises them that he will take good care of their dear friend.

The day the bride enters the new household, a special Havan is performed under the guidance of the family priest. The bride and the groom cook kheer (rice pudding) and it is served to all the assembled relatives who bless them. At the time of Feroni (the ritual return of the bride after her first visit from her father's house-also known as Dwiragaman) the bride and groom are welcomed with great joy and fed sweets and butter.

Wedding: At the time of the wedding, the Suhagi jewellery (denoting a girls married status) is presented by the Mama and the rest is given by the parents of the bride and the groom. The groom's family displays their gifts (Barasuhi) to the bride, to all assembled, so that they may judge their financial status. Among the poorer sections, the gifts and the cash to be given to the bride by her family at the time of the wedding are fixed in advance.

In the plains, the bride's brother presents the groom with a 'dhoti' and a ring and ushers him to the place where the marriage ceremony is to take place. In the areas of Kinnaur the bride's father presents the groom with a white turban and ties a sword or a dagger to his waist band to indicate the start of the ceremonies. All this time wine cups are also presented to both the match-maker and the groom. When the marriage party returns with the bride it is greeted by the fellow villagers holding torches. Goats are sacrificed and special rituals are performed to ward off evil spirits and ghosts.

Rituals Connected with Marriage: There are many rituals associated with the coming of a new bride into the family. The bride first performs the puja to the deities of her new family under the guidance of the older women and is then made to distribute sweets (Gune) in front of the Dehre which is a traditional wall painting done as a religious ritual after marriage.

The bride distributes the Gune with both hands. The groom is the first to get these and gives his bride, money or jewellery in return. Ritual songs are sung at this time by women sitting around the bride. Munh Dikhai is a custom which reveals the face of the bride. The mother-in-law comes first who presents the bride with jewellery and sees her face and then follows the uncles wives, sister-in-law etc. Each one of them presents the bride with money or pieces of jewellery.

Pair Bandai (touching the feet) is another custom which helps introduce the bride to husband's family. In this, the bride first offers the close relatives a gift of money and then covering her hands with the edge of her sari, touches their feet. She is then blessed by the elders to be well-loved of her husband and produce sons.

Darosh Dab Dhab, Dam-Chalshish, Dual or Har, Batta-Satta, Jhajhara, Gadar, Mool Biah, Jhindphook and Yuth Vivah are some other interesting forms of marriage prevalent in the area. Darosh Dab Dhab is a tribal system prevalent in Kinnaur. In this the girl is forcibly dragged away from a fair ground or a festival meeting. She pretends to scream, scratch, bite and show annoyance but the boy holding her does not relent his hold. At night the village tries to bring the girl round and if she agrees then the next day a match-maker goes to her family with a gift of five rupees and a bottle of wine (ijit) and tries to get their permission. Similar gifts are presented to the village deities.

In Dam-Chalshish, the lovers elope together and the boy's father sends the Mazomi to the girl's house and tries to placate them and their relatives with gifts. If the family agrees, then a ritual marriage follows. In Jhindphook, the lovers go to a lonely spot and set some shrubs on fire and then go round the fire seven times. This makes them husband and wife. In the Chalshish system as the girl departs from her home sad tunes are played and the son-in-law presents the mother of the daughter with a sum of five hundred rupees as Masore or the price of her milk.

Hari or Har means that a woman who is dissatisfied with her husband, goes and begins to live with another. Her new husband has to settle it with the previous one by offering him a price acceptable to him. Such marriages are known as Jhanjhara or Jhanhrada. The new husband also invites all his relatives and at night offers a special puja known as Nuala to lord Shiva. When the priest or the Chela gives him the lords blessings he in turn, puts his Balu (a piece of jewellery) on the Woman and this makes her his lawful wife. The Gaddis follow this custom more than the others.

The Gaddis and some labourer families follows the Batta-Satta system of marriage in which the bride's brother has to marry the groom's sister or vice versa. If one of the girls refuses to go to her husband, the other one also will stay back. In case of complications, the village assembly of Pachi (Panchayat) is called. They listen to arguments from both sides and give their verdict in writing, copies of which are preserved by both sides.

The Gaddis perform the marriage ceremony twice. First comes the Jooth Pana when the groom's party goes to the girl's house (who is usually a minor of 8-10 years) and breaks a lump of jaggery in the girl's name and the girls family smears them with red colour. On their way back, the groom's party distributes lumps of jaggery to all the passer by thus announcing the confirming of the betrothal. Then the real marriage ceremony follows, in which the woman from the girls family help her through the rituals.

There is no system of dowry. After five or ten years comes the second half known as Sadnoj. By now the girl is mature. On a fixed day the groom in ritual finery, goes to his wife's house with a few relatives and after staying there for a couple of days, departs with his bride for his own village. At this time gifts are presented and dances and celebrations begin in the groom's house to welcome the party.

In Pangi, at the time of the marriage the grooms younger brother presents the bride's mother with a silver rupee. This gives him the right of a second husband over the bride, but the bride is not to be shared by more than two brothers. The people in Pangi are monogamous and a widow may remarry, but such marriages are not held in high esteem.

Remarriage and the Sati: The higher castes do not allow the widows to remarry but the lower castes allow remarriage. In some cases after the death of the older brother, the younger one marries the widow. Some times the widow leaves her husband's house and moves in with someone. This is known as Ghar Karna (taking another house). Among the lower castes a woman may make four to five such changes of spouse in her lifetime. In such cases the new husband has to undertake the responsibilities for all the children born of previous marriages.

The Dehris (monuments) outside most villages are reminders of the prevalence of the system of Sati in which the widow burnt herself on the funeral pyre of her husband. Among the higher castes, the husbands presence is the only security for most woman. They observe a lot of fasts and perform many rituals to prolong their husband's life. Among them, even if widowed young, a women must suffer her widowhood till her dying day but may not take another husband.

Divorce: Some tribal communities have a divorce law known as Dehri, Hari or Har which is held above all the courts of law. In this the couple seeking divorce takes a twig of Shur Wood and snap it in front of witnesses and throw it behind them. In Lahaul a woolen thread is similarly snapped symbolising the termination of marital ties. In some villages the couple must break a sal leaf into two in the presence of fellow-villagers. In case of a divorce the woman forfeits all rights to the husband's property.

The Har and the Dehri systems decree that the party applying for divorce must pay compensation to the aggrieved party. Among the Gaddis this payment of compensation is known as giving Fargati. This is paid to the Numbadar (head) of the village who takes down the whole case in writing and settles the accounts peacefully. Due to the spread of literacy such divorces have decreased. People also choose mates more carefully now, which has reduced the risk of breakups. Most divorces have personal rather than financial causes. In some areas the divorce procedures are conducted by the Panchayat (village assembly) whose verdict is acceptable to both the parties.

Child Birth: The birth of a son is a great occasion in the villages. People light lamps and the women from the neighbourhood come and sing songs of joy and congratulations. The mother is treated with great reverence. The baby is delivered by old and experienced midwives who are paid both in cash and in kind.

In the Kinnaur area the palanquins of the gods are brought within their houses after a male child is delivered and a feast of rich food and liquor is given to the villagers. This custom is known as Shukud. At this time a goat may also be sacrificed. Among the Brahmins the Namkaran (the naming of the infant), Chudakaran (first snipping off of his locks) and Annaprashan (the first tasting of cereals by the baby) are all performed with great joy. In some areas in Solan, the infant is taken to a waterfall and lodged near it for the first three days. Getting a horoscope written for the baby is also a must. Marriages cannot be settled before the horoscopes of the couple have been matched properly.

At the time of child birth the mother is housed in a separate room. In the tribal areas she is lodged in a cattle-manor (Khudd). After delivery, the infant is bathed and wrapped in a clean cloth. The first twenty days are called Sootak and during this period the family observes abstention from all religious rituals. If touched by mistake, the idol is said to become polluted and an animal sacrifice becomes necessary to placate the god. Some other important ceremonies connected with child birth are the first sighting of the baby by the father and the first feeding of the tonic Ghutti to the infant. It is believed that the child imbibes the temperament of the person who gives him his first dose of Ghutti. Therefore the Ghutti is administered by some exceptionally good-natured member of the family.

After the twenty day Sootak period is over, the 'cleansing up' ceremony takes place. This occasion is celebrated with great fun. They call the ceremony Goontar and on this occasion special Sunds (sweet cookies) are made and distributed among the close relatives.

In the tribal areas, when a family is blessed with a son goats are sacrificed to the deities and the other fathers of boys in the village joyfully clobber the new father with chunks of meat. Money is also offered to the temples. The birth of a daughter is considered the beginning of heavy responsibilities and so only few celebrate it as joyous occasion. In some areas the girls from the village chase the girl's father round and round and he pretends to run away.

After the baby's birth and the casting of the horoscopes people make special efforts to propitiate the evil stars in the child's horoscope. For this, special Pujas are offered and alms are distributed. People hang little silver or copper Jantar (amulets) around the child's neck to ward off the bad effect of evil stars. Children born in the Gandmool hour are considered unlucky and are often gifted away ritually as soon as they are born.

When the child is seven months old he is given the first taste of cereal in the form of kheer (rice pudding). This ceremony is known as Kheerpoo. The child is fed kheer with a silver article shaped like the blade of grass. Female children are also fed kheer and special songs are sung. At this time a basket full of various things of daily use are also placed before the child. It is believed that the child shall pick up an article which fore-tells his future occupation.

Death: In Himachal the customs associated with death are quite strange and interesting. As death approaches, the sick man's body is lowered on the ground, smeared with fresh cow dung. His head must point to the north and as soon as death occurs, conch shells are blown. This is a signal for the relatives to burst out crying. It is inauspicious to die on a bed and alms must be given by the sick person prior to his or her death.

After the death has occurred, a linseed oil lamp with a cotton wick is lit and placed in a corner of the room and covered with a woven grass basket. This lamp symbolises the dead man. The mourners come and sit in this room and the ritual mourning is done here. The dead body is laid on plantain leaves in the courtyard, bathed and then placed in a wooden coffin or upon a bier and covered with a colourful shroud and taken to the cremation grounds. On the way, the funeral procession stops at a few places where some stones and leaves are placed in the name of the dead man.

Before consigning the body to the flames a Pind Dan (ritual feeding of balls made of cooked rice, sesame seeds and curds to the birds and elements in the name of the died one) is performed. It is considered propitious to add fuel wood to the pyre. After the cremation, people bathe and come back to the deceased's house. So long as the dead body lies within the house, no food can be cooked therein. After this for a month the close relatives observe Sootak. During this period the use of things like meat, fish, garlic, onions, asafoetida is taboo. At the end of this period either the daughter's or the son's father-in-law (Kudam) brings food items cooked with asafoetida and feeds it to the bereaved family, after this the taboo is lifted.

In some families, the death of an aged member is celebrated

with the slaying of goats and feasting. On the third day, the bones and ashes are immersed in a holy place like Haridwar, Rivalsar or Manasarovar. For ten days the house observes a mourning period. Mondays, Wednesdays, Thursdays and Fridays are taboo for condolence visits. The daughters come at the end of the month long Sootak. The close relatives have their heads shaven and the widow removes her marriage jewellery. On the tenth day clothes are washed (Kapad Dhulai) and the holy Garud Purana is recited by 'Charjee' (a special class that recites scriptures in houses where death has occurred). In the tribal families, the Lama reads out the scriptures. For a year each month the day of the death is observed with special rituals. A plaster statue of the dead one is placed near a stream and the articles of his use are immersed in the water.

If someone dies an untimely death a special ritual called Sapindi is performed. Each year an annual Shradda is performed to commemorate the dead one. Each four years a Chatur Varshik is done. People, usually Brahmins, numbering in three, fives, sevens, nines or elevens are invited and feasted and presented with pots and pans and clothes. The whole village is then feasted.

The tribal areas follow a slightly different set of customs. In Kinnaur when someone dies, all the villagers gather at his house at night. This custom is known as Drum Rating. The dead body is then bathed in a large vessel called Lam Kunyal and then wrapped up in a white shroud. Two people then carry the body to the cremation ground on a plank. The legs of the body are turned behind at the knees with the help of wooden pegs.

It is believed that if the legs are straight an evil spirit might enter the body. He also recites some Mantras and during this, it is considered auspicious if a drop of blood become visible on the forehead of the dead one. When the funeral procession leaves the house, a piece of bread stuffed with Dal is thrown on the roof top for the crows. It is believed that the crow can communicate with the dead person. For seven weeks, the Lama comes to the dead man's house to recite the sacred text (chhos). At the end of the seven week period the Lama and Jomo read the text together and are then fed by the family of the dead man. On the day of the death, the Lama tells them about life after death and about rebirth. Sometimes alms are given to counteract evil influences.

Some tribes light a lamp in the name of the dead one for seven days. On the third day after death the chholya ceremony is performed and on the thirteenth day Damkochang is performed. On the 15th day, the Lama performs a Havan. The next day, those who go to collect the ashes leave a stone or a little flag upon the hill top in the name of the dead one. A year after the death, the Lama performs the Fulyach (or the Dalhyang) ceremony, at which he gets food and clothes in the name of the dead.

These customs are followed with some local variations in the Lahaul valley. If an old man dies no one may touch the dead body till the Lama arrives at the house. The Lama whispers an invocation to the dead man's soul in his ear and ask it to leave the body and this is called 'Fuhan'. After this, the dead man is seated on a wooden or metal chair in a corner and a lamp is lit with butter in front of it. The body stays in the house for two or more days according to the status of the dead man's family.

Then it is wrapped in a shroud and placed on a bier and carried to the cremation ground. The Lama recites prayers, the relatives cry and conch shells are blown. Two men, one with a conch shell and another with a flag follow the funeral procession. Sometimes an umbrella is held over the bier. On the way, the procession stop a couple of times to allow the man with the flag and the man with the conch shell to circle the body for which they are paid a sum of money.

At the cremation ground, the shroud is torn into five pieces, four of which are hung upon the four corners of the funeral pyre and the fifth is placed on the forehead of the dead one. The

Lama recites mantras and gets barley, rice and butter thrown into the pyre which is set to light. On the next day the ashes are collected by the family and it is immersed in the Chandrabhaga river.

In the tribal areas some customs are quite unusual. In the Spiti valley when someone dies, the Jhanvan (witch doctor) is called to find out whether the body should be burnt, buried or cut up into pieces and thrown upon hill tops for the wild animals to consume. All communities there follow the orders of the Jhanvan. The Sanglas and the Sipis have their own customs.

COMMON CUSTOMS

The Thoda and the Buhana: The Thoda custom which probably originated in the Pauranic past, can be seen in the village fairs in the tribal areas. This is a competition in archery in the memory of the Pandavas. In this the interested parties form two teams, one called Pashi and other Sathi. The players then shoot arrows at spots marked near the feet. If the arrow hits the target the player jumps up and names one of the five pandava brothers.

The Buhana custom is a beautiful example of community feelings within the farming communities. In some area this is also known as Hela or Jwari. The planting of seedlings, weeding, hoeing and harvesting are all community activities here, and are performed co-operatively. This custom is beneficial to the smaller and poorer farmers whose necessary chores are thus completed on time without expense. While the tasks are being performed by the entire community for one of their brethren, a drummer stands at a raised spot and beats his drum rhythmically to which all keep time as they go about their work. At the end of the day's work all the workers are fed on Bhatedus (thick round bread made of whole wheat flour) and other delicacies. The women also work with the men and sing to the beat of the drum.

The Thatha: This is a custom prevalent in the Kinnaur

region and is designed to ward off the evil spirits and ghosts. Even the poorest families celebrate it once in every three or four years. In this, one hundred and eight clay lamps are lit, which symbolically dispel the darkness for the coming period. Then the Lama comes and performs a special puja in the house to the gods known as Vikyu.

The Bhoonda: The custom was largely prevalent in Mahasu and Kulu regions and seems to have its earliest roots in human sacrifice performed every twelve years. The last Bhoonda (at Vibhai in the Sutlej valley) is said to have been performed in the following manner

A man belonging to the Beda community was chosen for the ceremony, a few days prior to it. For three months he was housed in the village temple with great respect. During this period, he wove a rope with grass-measuring some four to five hundred Hath (a Hath is the length between the elbow and the tip of the middle finger of a mature human arm). On the fixed day a procession of the gods was brought out ceremoniously.

The Beda led this procession holding aloft an umbrella made of blue cloth, and supported on each side by his two wives. He wore only one article of clothing and a red thread around his neck. As the precession reached the spot where the Bhoonda was to be performed one end of the grass rope was tied to the pillar on the top of the hill and the other to another pillar, at the bottom of the same hill. The procession then took the Beda into the temple and sacrifices a goat.

In the temple the Beda was offered to the gods and then the procession returned to the spot where the Bhoonda was to be performed. Here on the top of the hill a woolen seat was laid on the rope with bags of sand suspended on both sides to keep it balanced. The Bhoonda was seated on that and at a signal from the priest he was pushed down hill. The seat flew down with the Beda. His survival depended purely on chance. If the Beda survives he is paid a sum of some 80/-to 90/-rupees from the temple fund. The observers also give him money. The last

Bhoonda took place in 1902 at a village near Nirat. The custom is nearly obsolete now.

Tana Mana: This is a custom designed to stop the spread of epidemics in a village and is prevalent in the villages along the Indo-Tibetan border. When anyone in these areas contracts a contagious disease and is critically ill, a locally available boulder of white stone is put at his door steps at a spot where any one may see it and know that some one within the house is lying ill with a contagious disease.

Due to the taboos this custom enforces, in order to isolate the patient, even the doctors are not allowed into the patients rooms. The entrance to each village in the area is guarded to check the entry of some one suffering from the disease. Between the villages of Raja and Kibbar, each person that enters the area has to be checked by the Lama against contagious diseases.

The Doom: A revolt by the subject of a particularly cruel or ruthless local Rana or Raja is known as 'Doom'. To attract the royal attention to their grievances the people in the area struck work and departed peacefully into the nearby forest, which brought all activity in the region to a standstill and forced the ruler to take measures to redress their grievances. This custom was always followed peacefully and there was no violence of any kind.

Sacrifices: Animal sacrifices are performed in order to reap a good harvest or to save a good crop from destruction by the evil forces. When the crop is ready for harvesting, a black goat is led around the fields and sacrificed. The meat of the goat is then distributed in the village as a holy 'prasad of the gods'. Sometimes to propitiate Yakshas, saints, goddesses or family gods, people perform a Jatra. In this a whole family along with all its numerous relatives leaves in a procession to the temple of the deity all dressed up, singing devotional songs. They carry along with them foodstuff of all kinds and the sacrificial goat. The drummer and the flag are also a part of the procession. As the women folk sing Jatra songs along the way, an old woman makes little signs on the road, shaped like footprints. These are known as 'Leekhnu'.

As the procession reaches the deity's temple, first the puja is performed and then all the family members sprinkle water on the sacrificial goat and at the same time urging the deity to accept the gift of the animal. When the animal gives his body a shake, it is taken as a sigh from the deity signifying his acceptance.

If the goat does not shiver, it is taken to be a sign of the deity's wrath and people begin praying. When the ritual is over the goat is sacrificed.

The meat is then cooked and served. The party spends the night in the temple premises singing songs and asking questions about sickness and crops of the devotees on whom the spirit of the deity is said to descend. In the morning after offering puja the group comes back to the village.

Earlier it was customary to perform a human sacrifice at the time of the building of a canal, a water tank or a bridge. But this is obsolete now and animal sacrifice has replaced human sacrifice. Some people who object to bloodshed offer sweets and other articles to the deity.

In Malana (Kulu) and Dodra Kwar (Mahasu) the twin deities Jamlu and Mahasu are unquestionably considered as the rulers of the area. Nothing is done here without consulting them and obtaining their permission.

At the time of harvesting, feasts are offered to the deities especially to Baba. Trees are also considered holy. On fast days the women folk worship the Peepal, the Banyan, the Mango and the Pomegranate trees and offer clothes and all kinds of delicacies to them. The Banyan tree is worshipped on the day of the Vata Savitri fast. The pomegranate tree is worshipped at the time of weddings. Friendships are also formed beneath this tree by formally appointing the trees as the witness. When the new grains have been harvested, young virgins (kanya) are fed and relatives feasted and certain traditional delicacies like kheer and halwa are cooked.

The Fasts: Women fast on the first (Sankranti), the eleventh (Ekadashi) and the fifteenth day of the full moon (Poornima). Among the higher castes fasting by women is taken to guarantee prolonged prosperity and physical well-being among the family members. Giving up a fast after a fixed period, is known as 'Mokh'.

On the day of a fast the women clean the house and paint ritual 'Lekhnu' on the floor and then collect all the required articles for the particular fast and offer puja to the deity. Unmarried girls are also supposed to fast on the full moon day. On the 'Sankranti' day the Brahmin priests visit their clients who give them alms according to their means.

Treating House Guests: As the guest arrives he is offered a bed, food, a hookah and a tea. He is looked upon as an incarnation of the gods. If he comes on the day of festival he must not leave without having a meal. Visiting relatives and married daughters must not be sent back without gifts of sweets and clothes. The guests also never arrive empty handed. If they can manage nothing else, they bring some fruits for the hosts. The women embrace each other when departing and touch the feet of the elders. Married daughters and children are also given gifts of money. The married daughters often weep at leaving their fathers house after a visit.

In some areas the customs for welcoming a guest are very strange. In Chachyot area when the guest reaches a house the family does not open the door to him. Neither they come out or offer him a seat. The guest lets himself in and finds a seat. In a little while the host family files in and welcomes him. His feet are bathed with warm water and he is given delicacies to eat. The guest as also the married daughter's husband are called Prahuna.

Before a wedding or a sacred thread ceremony for a boy, the boy and the bride-to-be are invited specially and presented with gifts. This custom is known as Lodhak. The relatives cook many delicacies at this time and send it for the bride and the groom. Special foods are offered to them and songs are sung. The gifts bestowed by the relatives on this occasion are to be remembered and returned when a similar occasion arises in the other houses. This custom promotes mutual good-will and co-operation.

Untouchability has fossilized in the area into a rigid and ugly custom. The untouchables may not talk direct to someone from a high caste, use their wells or enter their houses with shoes on. They must leave the road if a man from a high caste is passing by and in wedding feasts they cannot sit with every one else. They are served food on leaves which they must accept after repeated bowings and they must remove the carcasses of dead animals from the village for which they are paid in kind at the time of the harvesting season.

PEOPLE AND CULTURE

Around 96% of the population of the state is of Hindus. The major communities includes Brahmins, Rajputs, Choudharies, Kannets, Rathis and Kolis. The tribal population comprises the Gaddis, Kinnars, gadoun,(jadoun) Tanolis. Gujjars, Pangawals and Lahaulis. From the alpine pasture regions to the lower regions during the cold winter season are mainly Hindus. The Kinnars are the inhabitants of Kinnaur and they generally practice polyandry and polygamy. The Gujjars are nomadic people who rear buffalo herds and are mainly Muslim. The Lahaulis of Lahaul and Spiti and native of spiti, Kinnaur region mainly comprises Buddhists. A percentage of people are also Tibetans. Muslim, Christian and Sikhs are in minority but they also enjoy the same rights as Hindus.

Though Hindi is the state language, many people speak the various Western Pahari languages. A majority of the population is engaged in agricultural practices, however the more educated of them are now moving towards tertiary sectors. As per the traditional dressing norms the dress of the Brahmin male includes dhoti, kurta, coat, waistcoat, turban and a hand towel while that of the Rajput male consists of tight fitting churidar pyjamas, a long coat and a starched turban. With the changing time the dress up of the people has now become a mixed one.

Though the above-mentioned style is now hardly followed, people have started wearing western style of clothes.

The typical house is constructed of clay bricks and the roofs are of slate. In some areas the slate roof is also replaced by timber.

Arts and crafts

The handicraft that comes out of this state are the carpets, leather works, shawls, paintings, metalware, woodwork and paintings. Pashmina shawl is the prity product which is highly in demand not only in Himachal but all over the country. Colourful Himachali caps are also famous art work of the people. A tribe namely *Dom* is expert in manufacturing bamboo items like boxes, sofas, chairs, baskets and rack. Metalware of the state include utensils, ritualistic vessels, idols, gold and silver jewelleries.

Weaving, carving, painting, or chiselling is considered to be the part of the life of *Himachalis*. Himachal is well known for designing shawls especially in Kullu. The architecture, objects, shops, museums, galleries and craftsmen charm with the variety perfected through time.

Women take an active part in pottery and men in carpentry. For ages, wood is used in Himachal in the construction of temples, homes, idols etc.

Music and dance

Music and dance of Himachal Pradesh reflects its cultural identity. Through their dance and music, they entreat their gods during local festivals and other special occasions. There are also dances that are specific to certain regions of the state.

Some of the dance forms of Himachal are *Losar Shona Chuksam*(Kinnaur), *Dangi* (Chamba), *Gee Dance* and *Burah dance*, (Sirmour), *Naati, Kharait, Ujagjama and Chadhgebrikar* (Kullu) and *Shunto* (Lahaul & Spiti).

People of the state generally prefer folk music. There is no classical form of music, as for the Himachal Pradesh is concerned.

Himachali dance forms are highly varied and quite complicated. These dances are very vital part of the tribal life. It reflects the culture and the tradition of Himachal Pradesh. Hardly any festivity here is celebrated without dancing. Some of the dance forms like *Dulshol, Dharveshi, Drodi, Dev Naritya, Rakshas Nritya, Dangi, Lasa, Nati* and *Nagas* are danced all over the region.

Fairs and festivals

Photo: Kullu Dussehra

Apart from the fairs and festivals that are celebrated all over India, there are number of other fairs and festivals also that are at the high point of Himachal Pradesh. These festivals are the time for the *Himachalis* to adorn colourful dress and accessories and get mixed up with the rest of their *kins*. Some of these fairs and festivals in the upper regions are the Kullu Dussehra, Shivratri Fair (Mandi), Shoolini Mela (Solan), *Minjar Fair* (Chamba), Mani Mahesh Chhari Yatra (Chamba), Renuka fair (Sirmaur), Lavi Trade Fair (Rampur), Vrajeshwari fair (Kangra), Jwalamukhi Fair (Jwalamukhi), Holi Fair (Sujanpur Tira), and Naina Devi Fair (Bilaspur),Fulaich {Kinnaur valley}. In the lower regions of Himachal are temple Fairs in Una District such as the *Peeplo* Fair, the 'Mairi' Guruduwara Fair, the 'Chintpurni' temple Fair, the 'Kamakhya temple' Fair, including the annual *Himachal Hill Festival* in the village *Polian Purohitan* during the fourth week of October. The centuries old Sair festival is celebrated mainly in Shimla, Mandi, Kullu and Solan districts every year in mid-September. It is celebrated to mark the end of the crop harvest and also the rakhi thread are removed and offered to the mother sairi.

Cuisine

Pachole

The day-to-day food of *Himachalis* is very similar to that of the rest of north India. They too have lentil, broth, rice, vegetablesand bread. As compared to other states in north India non-vegetarian cuisine is preferred. Traditionally, Himachali cuisine is dominated by red meat and wheat bread. Thick and rich gravy, with aromatic spices, is used in abundance as the base of many dishes. Now, steamed momos (dumplings) and noodles are also readily available and popular with travellers who want to graduate to Indian food slowly. Some of the specialities of Himachal include *Manee, Mandra* or "Madra", "Palda", "Redu" *Patode, Chouck, Bhagjery* and *chutney* of til(sesame seeds).

LAND AND THE PEOPLE

Himachal Pradesh formerly the Punjab Hill States, is a mostly mountainous state in northern India. Neighbouring regions are Tibet to the east, Jammu and Kashmir to the north and northwest, Punjab to the southwest, Haryana and Uttar Pradesh to the south and Uttarakhand to the southeast. With an area of 55,658 km^2 (21,490 sq mi), Himachal is one of the smaller states of the country and holds the 17th rank in the list of States and Union Territories of India.

The state capital is Shimla (formerly British India's summer capital under the name Shimla), other major towns are Solan, Dharamsala, Kangra, Mandi, Kullu, Chamba, Hamirpur, Dalhousie and Manali. The western Himalayas lie in the north and east and the smaller Shiwalik (or Shivalik) range in the south. Himachal Pradesh has five major rivers. These are the Sutlej, Ravi, Chenab, Beas and Yamuna.

LAND

Himachal Pradesh, spread over 55,673 sq. km. is bordered by Jammu and Kashmir on north, Punjab on west and southwest, Haryana on south Uttaranchal on south-east and by Tibet on the east. It is a mountainous region, known for the natural beauty of its forests, rivers, valleys, hills and dales and is rich in natural resources. The state is located in altitudes ranging from 450 meters to 6500 meters above sea level. It is veiled from the plains by the Shivalik range of mountains. (Shivalik literally means the tresses of Lord Shiva). There is a general increase in elevation from west to east and from south to north. The physiographic divisions from south to north are (1) The outer Himalayas or the Shivaliks (2) The lesser Himalayas or the central zone (3) The great Himalayan and Zaskar or the northern zone.

The Shivaliks consist of lower hills (about 600 mtrs above sea level). These hills are composed of highly unconsolidated deposits which causes a high rate of erosion and deforestation. The lesser Himalayas are marked by a gradual elevation towards the Dhauladhar and the Pir Panjal ranges. The rise is more abrupt in the Shimla hills, to the south of which is the high peak of church-Chandni (3647 mtrs). North of river Sutlej, the rise is gradual.

The Kangra valley is a longitudinal trough at the foot of the Dhauladhar range. Dhauladhar which means the 'White Peak' has a mean elevation of about 4550 meters. It has an abrupt rise of 3600 mtrs above the Kangra valley. The largest of the lesser Himalayan ranges, the Pir Panjal, branches off from the greater Himalayan range near the bank of the river Sutlej. Numerous glaciers exist and several passes lie across Pir Panjal. The Rohtang Pass (4800 mtrs) is one of them.

The great Himalayan range (5000-6000 meters) runs along the eastern boundary and is cut across by the Sutlej. Some of the famous passes in this range are Kangla (5248 mtrs), Bara Lacha (4512 mtrs), Parang (5548 mtrs) and Pin Parbati (4802 mtrs).

The Zaskar range is the eastern most range and separates Kinnaur and Spiti from Tibet. It has peaks rising over 6500 mtrs, Shilla (7026 mtrs) and Riwo Phargyul (6791 mtrs) are the highest among its peaks. There are many glaciers or Shigri (local name) over the Zaskar and the great Himalayan ranges.

Himachal has rich flora. Forests cover about 38% of the area. Several varieties of vegetation from the Himalayan meadows and high altitude birch and down to the tropical shrub and bamboo forests of the low foot hills are found here. It has a variety of wild life too. Himachal has 49 cities and towns. The smallest town is Naina Devi and the largest is Shimla with a population of about 6,17,404. Urban population is only 7.5% of the total population. Most of the people live in rural habitations varying in size from isolated hamlets to conglomerated settlements.

PEOPLE

Scores of races, communities and cultures have intermingled in Himachal. The crime rate is very low. There faiths are simple, beliefs primitive and myths difficult to fathom. A birth, a fair, a community gathering, a marriage, a festival all provide them opportunity for song and dance. Their has been relatively a closed society. They hardly ever lock up their houses. There are few instances of theft or trickery. They firmly believe that all their act whether good or bad are recorded in heaven and their proportions, shall eventually decide their next birth.

Ninety three percent of the state population are engaged in agriculture. Most of the land is owned by Rajputs, Brahmins and Mahajans (the high caste) who dominate the economic and political life of the state. They dominate in ritual status too. The low castes who form about 24% of the population are mostly artisans. They depend on the high castes for their livelihood and hold them in respect. The relationship is gradually changing to interdependence with the implementation of social and agrarian reforms.

The people of Himachal love colour. Their dress patterns follow the local climate. The people of Lahaul wear long gowns and trousers but their gowns do not have mandarin sleeves. They wear grass or leather boots. Their caps indicate the region they come from.

Castes: The Rajputs are in a majority in Himachal. They are the descendants of immigrant Rajputs who came here to establish small princely states or who were driven to the hills by the Muslim invaders. The earlier inhabitants, the Khasia (descendants of the Khasas) joined the Rajputs and adopted some of their sub-castes. But a certain distance has always persisted in their social relationship. Rajputs are mostly landed people and are engaged in agriculture. They are also good soldiers. In relation to its population Himachal has contributed the maximum number of Rajputs to the Indian army. The Rajputs soldiers from Kangra and Hamispur areas are well known for their qualities of bravery and loyalty. Kotoch, Bana,

Pathaniya and Baliriye are the main branches of the Rajputs in the area. The Kanait Rajputs are considered a little below these and they have taken to farming.

The Brahmins, who were the priests of Rajputs are the second largest group. Shrotriyas, the Dixit, the Nagas, the Panch Karmas and the Padhes are some prominent Brahmin branches. They have more influence in the lower hills than in the higher regions.

The Ghirats are next in number. They are the descendants of Kirats according to some sources. But according to ethnographic evidence they are of Indo-Aryan origin. They are farmers.

Mahajans and Soods, the business communities are sprinkled all over. They wield great influence even though they are a small minority. They have a shop in almost every village right up to the Tibetan border. Traditionally they used to be the main exporters and importers of the products in the state. Now cooperatives and corporations are taking up their role.

Chahang, Saini etc. are other castes where people are professional farmers. The Ahirs own windmills and catch fish. The Darai have settled along the river Beas. Their forefathers were boatmen. Lohar (ironsmiths), Tarkhan (carpenter), Nai (barbers), Dusali, Doomna, Chamar (cobblers) and Julahas (weavers) follow their paternal professions.

The educated in these castes are moving towards other professions and also into farming. The caste system has weakened and there is a greater intermingling among the people in the society. The untouchables are being specially protected and helped by the government by special acts. A few peasant families belong to the backward classes. All these castes are divided into the categories of Kachha, Pakka, Nagar Kotiya and Bhatedu.

Language: Hindi is the state language but people mostly converse in 'Pahari'. This language has various dialects or sub-languages. Grierson in his linguistic survey had called it 'Western Pahari' and had demarcated its area from Jainsar

Bawar in the Uttar Pradesh hills (near Dehra Dun) to Bhadarwah in Jammu and Kashmir. The various dialects of Pahari spoken in the region are Mandiali (in Mandi), Kulavi (in Kulu), Kehluri (in Bilaspur), Hinduri (in Nalagarh), Chameali (in Chamba), Sirmauri (in Sirmur), Miahasvi (in Mahasu region) and Pangwali (in Pangi). Besides, there are the dialects of Bhot orgin, the Kinnauri, the Lahauli and the Spitian. All dialects of Pahari are of Sanskritic origin. They have been written differently in different times. In earlier days they were written in 'Tankri' or 'Thahau', but later during the Muslim period they were written in the Persian script and then again in Devanagiri.

Dress: Dhoti, kurta, coat, waistcoat, turban (or cap), a hand towel upon the shoulders and a copy of the Panchang (astrological ephemeris) under the arm are the traditional attire of the Brahmin priest. The Rajputs wore tight fitting churidar pyjamas, a long coat, a starched turban with a special crown, pointed shoes, a flourishing pair of moustaches and a frown upon their foreheads. The Rajputs followed the Purdah system. Their wives and daughters when they stepped out of the house, rode in curtained palanquins.

They lived in close proximity to each other and had special guest houses, a little removed from their dwelling places. Women belonging to the Brahmin and the Rajput families wore kurtas, salwars, long skirts (ghaghri), embroidered tops (choli) and red head scarves (rahide) with gold edgings. The farmers and labour classes wore only kurta, a loincloth and a cap. They put on long pyjamas only on special occasions like a wedding or a festival. The new socioeconomic trends have changed all this classes and castes now wear western style clothes.

Houses: The houses are built of clay bricks and the roofs are of slate. In the hill areas stones are used instead of bricks and timber is used for the roofs. The cattle houses are close to the house. People prefer pucca houses. The tribals live in double storeyed houses where the ground floor is used for the cattle and the first floor is used as their living quarters. The labourers live in thatched huts. The architectural patterns change from area to area.

Among the gods both Aryan and non-Aryan gods are worshipped. Shiva is the chief god among the Gaddis. Vishnu, Krishna and Buddha are also worshipped. There is very little impact of Jainism. The Buddhist Lama religion has had a great impact in the Lahaul, Spiti, Pangi and Kinnaur areas.

TRIBES

The tribal population constitute the Kinners or Kinnaure, the Lahules, the Spitians, the Pangwalas, the Gaddis and the Gujjars. Their permanent and semipermanent dwelling places are in Kinnaur, Lahaul. Pangi and Gadderan (Chamba and Bharmaur). They have their own customs, traditions, religious beliefs, dances and music. Most of these tribes are nomadic but they are immensely popular due to their open and friendly temperament.

Most tribals love to drink although the higher castes consider drinking sinful. There are three main meals in the morning (Nuhari), noon (Dhupahari) and evening (Sanhiyalu). The wedding feast is known as Datayalu. A traditional meal consists of boiled rice, Roti (unleavened bread), curried dal, buttermilk and vegetables.

In the hill areas Roti made of barley or corn is popular. The Kangra people eat more rice. Sweet fritters (Gulgule) are made for birthdays and savouries (Polu Pakodu) during the Shradhas. There are special courses for special occasions. All these tribes are very fond of silver ornaments. The women wear strings of beads and corals.

Kinnaure: The Kinners or Kinnaure inhabit the border district of Kinnaur. Physically they are closer to the Aryan races in their tall well-built bodies, their high foreheads, large eyes and fair complexions.

Temperamentally they are a gentle and soft-spoken people, quite content to live in poverty. Their main occupation is rearing sheep and goats and raising wool. Some are engaged in agriculture and horticulture. They live in joint families and men and women have more than one mate.

Their marriage customs are very interesting. All the brothers in a family share a wife.

They call it the Pandava marriage. Due to this a lot of girls remain unmarried. But these systems are being abandoned in the changing socioeconomic conditions.

Some say they are the descendants of the Kinners of Mahabharata fame but others believe them to be remnants of Kirats who were first defeated by the Aryans and then pushed by the Khasaa to remote areas in the trans-Himalayan region. Their mongoloid features are evidence of the intermixing of ideas on the borders.

Kinnaur women are beautiful, modest and homely and spend most of their time in the fields. A Kinnaur girl unable to find suitable match becomes a Jomo (a Buddhist nun). Men wear long coats (chubha) and woolen pyjamas (chamu sutan) and women Dhoru (a kind of woolen saree). Their shoes are made of wool and goat hair. They wear Bushahri cape. They are fond of meat and drink home-distilled wine 'Angoori'.

Lahule: The word Lahule means the dwellers of Lahaul. The aboriginal Lahaules are a mixture of the aboriginal Munda tribe and the racially intermixed Tibetans. Lahules are enterprising.

Besides farming they are engaged in trade. Their valley lies on the traditional trade routes to Ladakh, Sinkrang and beyond. They carried wheat from the plains, and their own barley to Tibet. Now that Tibet is closed to them, they export 'Kuth' (a herb used in medicine) to Kolcuta for onward dispatch to foreign markets.

Lahules are divided into upper and lower classes. Their higher castes are those of Brahmins and Thakurs. They also have Lohars and Dagis. Their chief religion is Buddhism. Each well-to-do family has its own shrine with a statue of the Buddha in it. Their chief temple is Trilokinath. They are a colourful people and their women adorn their dresses with ornaments. They marry within their tribe and a woman can have more than one mate. Divorce is recognised and simple.

Piral: The goatherds are called Piral. They are nomads. In the winter month they come down to Kangra and the forests of Hoshiarpur and in the summer they live along the banks of the rivers Chandrabhaga in Lahaul. They are brave and hard working and love festivities of all kinds. Their marriage customs are similar to those of the Hindus. Some of them follow polygamy.

Gaddis: The Gaddis live in the Chamba-Sirmaur regions. Their settlements are known as Gadderan which means the abode of the Gaddis. Gaddis are descendants of the Khatris of Punjab who migrated to the high hill due to persecution by the Muslim rulers.

This tribe has also settled in Mandi, Kangra and Bilaspur but their largest numbers live in the Kamgra district. Some of their main castes and sub-castes are Brahmins, Khatris, Rajputs, Thakurs, Rathis, Kolis, Sippys, Lohars, Bahdis and Hali. The Khatris and Rajputs wear Chola and Dora (the sacred thread) according to the Gaddi custom. When taking decisions about marriage they consider the Gotra. The Gaddi dress is very attractive. Their black sash is very helpful in carrying weight upon the back. Their women wear colourful homespun dresses and a thick scarf over their heads which can also be used as a veil. They often carry little kids in the folds of their special sashes. The Gaddi women wear several rows of semi precious stones and display little mirrors which are studded in the necklaces. They use peacock feathers as ornaments.

The Gaddis are shepherds. Their sheep and goats are known as Dhan (property). Some of them do farming also and some families are weavers and tinkers by trade. Before the advent of the machines they also earned their living by pounding millet and carrying loads. Financially they are well off. Their traditional attire consists of a long coat (chola), dora, safa (turban), nualali tope (cap) and a draping sheet. They are fond of tobacco and in the wedding feasts wine is also served.

The Gaddis spend half of the year in their villages cultivating their fields and the remaining half migrating in search of grass and fodder for their herds. They are simple and virtuous and live in joint families and have a strict moral code. Their women are modest and chaste.

Nepalese: The houses of the Nepalese who had settled in the state are small, surrounded by gardens and full of decorative articles. Most of them are in the armed forces. Their women wear saris and love to wear flowers round their necks, in their hair and their ears. Dharmashala (Mcleod-Gunj) has a large number of Tibetan refuges settlement. Their dress, food habits and speech are different from the local people. They are mostly traders by profession.

3

Government and Politics

GOVERNMENT

The Legislative Assembly of Himachal Pradesh has no pre-Constitution history. The State itself is a post-Independence creation. It came into being as a centrally administered territory on 15 April 1948 from the integration of thirty erstwhile princely states.

Town Hall in Shimla

Himachal Pradesh is governed through a parliamentary system of representative democracy, a feature the state shares with other Indian states. Universal suffrage is granted to residents. The legislature consists of elected members and special office bearers such as the Speaker and the Deputy Speaker who are elected by the members. Assembly meetings are presided over by the Speaker or the Deputy Speaker in the Speaker's absence. The judiciary is composed of the Himachal Pradesh High Court and a system of lower courts. Executive authority is vested in the Council of Ministers headed by the Chief Minister, although the titular head of government is the Governor. The Governor is the head of state appointed by the President of India. The leader of the party or coalition with a majority in the Legislative Assembly is appointed as the Chief Minister by the Governor, and the Council of Ministers are appointed by the Governor on the advice of the Chief Minister. The Council of Ministers reports to the Legislative Assembly. The Assembly is unicameral with 68 Members of the Legislative Assembly (MLA). Terms of office run for 5 years, unless the Assembly is dissolved prior to the completion of the term. Auxiliary authorities known as *panchayats*, for which local body elections are regularly held, govern local affairs.

In the assembly elections held in November 2017, the BJP secured an absolute majority. The BJP won 44 of the 68 seats while the Congress won only 21 of the 68 seats. Jai Ram Thakur was sworn-in as Himachal Pradesh's Chief Minister for the first time in Shimla on 27 December 2017.

PROTECTED AREAS OF HIMACHAL PRADESH

Forests in the state of Himachal Pradesh (northern India) currently cover an area of nearly 37,691 square kilometres (14,553 sq mi), which is about 38.3% of the total land area of the state. The forests were once considered to be the main source of income of the state and most of the original forests were clear felled. The emphasis has shifted, however, from exploitation to conservation. The state government aims to increase forest cover to 50% of the total land area. There have been various projects, including the establishment of protected areas such as National Parks, designed to preserve and expand the forests.

Preservation and nationalisation of forests

Steps are being taken to intensify environmental preservation and sustainable development in the Himachal Pradesh region. All remaining forests in Himachal Pradesh have been nationalised under the supervision of the officers like Indian forest service, Himachal Forest Service and seasoned Range/Dy.Range Forest Officers.Felling of trees and sale of timber is now controlled by the State Forest Corporation, and an *Enforcement Organisation* has been established to prevent the illegal felling of trees and the smuggling of timber. Hunting has also been restricted.

The government has created 33 Sanctuaries, two National Parks. Additional national parks sites are proposed.

Reafforestation programs

A World Bank assisted *Social Forestry Project* has been launched. The aim of the project is to plant more trees for fuel, fodder, and timber to meet the basic requirements of the local people, thus avoiding depletion of the old growth forests. The deforested *Kandi* areas are also being reafforested in another project financially assisted by the World Bank.

GOVERNMENT OF HIMACHAL PRADESH

The Government of Himachal Pradesh also known as the State Government of Himachal Pradesh, or locally as State Government, is the supreme governing authority of the Indian state of Himachal Pradesh. It consists of an executive branch, led by the Governor of Himachal Pradesh, a judiciary and a legislative branch.

Like other states in India, the head of state of Himachal Pradesh is the Governor, appointed by the President of India on the advice of the Central government. His or her post is largely ceremonial. The Chief Minister is the head of government and is vested with most of the executive powers. Shimla is the capital of Himachal Pradesh, and houses the Vidhan Sabha (Legislative Assembly) and the secretariat (Ellersile). The Himachal Pradesh high court is located in Shimla, which has jurisdiction over the whole of Himachal Pradesh. The present Legislative Assembly of Himachal Pradesh is unicameral.

State administrative structure

State administrative structure

Administrative structure (2002)	Numbers
Districts	12
Tehsils	75
Subdivisions	52
Blocks	75
Villages	20118
Towns	57
Constituencies	**Numbers**
Lok Sabha	4
Rajya Sabha	3
Assembly constituencies	68

The Himachal Pradesh Legislative Assembly has no pre-Constitution history. The state itself is a post-independence creation. It first came into being as a centrally administered territory on 15 April 1948 by the integration of 30 erstwhile princely states.

Himachal Pradesh is governed through a parliamentary system of representative democracy, a feature the state shares with other Indian states. Universal suffrage is granted to residents.

The legislature of Himachal Pradesh is unicameral and at present, the Assembly has a strength of 68. The tenure of the Assembly is five years unless it is sooner dissolved. There are 14 House Committees in the Assembly.

In the assembly elections held in November 2012, the Congress secured an absolute majority. The Congress won 36 of the 68 seats while the BJP won 26 of the 68 seats. Virbhadra Singh was sworn in as Himachal Pradesh's Chief Minister for a record sixth term in Shimla on 25 December 2012. Virbhadra Singh, who has held the top office in Himachal five times in the past, was administered the oath of office and secrecy by Governor Urmila Singh at an open ceremony at the historic Ridge Maidan in Shimla.

ADMINISTRATIVE DIVISIONS

The state of Himachal Pradesh is divided into 12 districts which are grouped into three divisions, Shimla, Kangra and Mandi. The districts are further divided into 69 subdivisions, 78 blocks and 145 Tehsils.

Divisions	Districts
Kangra	Chamba, Kangra, Una
Mandi	Bilaspur, Hamirpur, Kullu, Lahaul and Spiti, Mandi
Shimla	Kinnaur, Shimla, Sirmaur, Solan

Administrative Structure

Divisions	3
Districts	12
Tehsils/ Sub-Tehsils	169
Developmental Blocks	78
Urban Local Bodies	49
Towns	59
Gram Panchayats	3226
Villages	20690
Police Stations	127
Lok Sabha Seats	4
Rajya Sabha Seats	3
Assembly Constituencies	68

POLITICS OF HIMACHAL PRADESH

The key political players in Himachal Pradesh state in north-west India are the ruling Indian National Congress and Bharatiya Janata Party.

National politics

There are four Lok Sabha (lower house of the Indian Parliament) constituencies in Himachal Pradesh.

State politics

The Himachal Pradesh Legislative Assembly has 68 seats who are directly elected from single-seat constituencies.

LIST OF POLITICAL PARTIES

All India Tribes and Minorities Front: All India Tribes and Minorities Front is a political party in the Indian state of Himachal Pradesh. The party works for the issues affecting the adivasi population. The party president is Mangal Singh Negi.

AITMF advocates United Nations involvement as mediators in the Kashmir issue. The party also advocates a trifurcation of the state of Jammu and Kashmir in Kashmir, Jammu and Ladakh.

Him Loktantrik Morcha

Him Loktantrik Morcha, a political front in the Indian state of Himachal Pradesh. HLM was formed ahead of the 2002 Shimla Municipal Corporation elections, as an alternative to both Indian National Congress and Bharatiya Janata Party. The convenor of HLM was Mohinder Singh Chaudhury. The front consisted of Communist Party of India (Marxist), the Janata Dal (Secular), the Lok Janshakti Party, the Samajwadi Party and a few secular regional parties.

Following dissatisfaction over Singh's move to make HLM into a political party, Samajwadi Party, Samajwadi Janata Party (Rashtriya) and Janata Dal (Secular) formed the *Himachal Jan Morcha* (Himalyana People's Front) in October 2002.

Singh later registered Loktantrik Morcha (Himachal Pradesh) as a political party.

Himachal Kranti Party

Himachal Kranti Party (Himalayan Revolution Party), a political party in the Indian state of Himachal Pradesh. HKP was formed after the 1998 state assembly elections, when two Himachal Vikas Congress members of the assembly, Mansa Ram and Prakash Chaudhary, split to form HKP. HKP merged with Bharatiya Janata Party in 1999.

A party with the same name contested the 1993 state assembly elections.

Himachal Vikas Congress

Himachal Vikas Congress, was a regional political party in Himachal Pradesh, India. HVC was formed when Sukh Ram split from the Indian National Congress. HVC merged with Congress in 2004.

Janhit Morcha

Janhit Morcha is a political party in India founded in 2002 by Vidya Sagar (ex-Agriculture Minister of Himachal Pradesh), who had broken away from BJP. In the state legislative assembly elections in Himachal Pradesh 2003 Vidya Sagar stood as a candidate in Kangra. He came third with 9 882 votes (20,41%). It is unclear whether the party still exists or if it has reunified with BJP.

Lok Raj Party Himachal Pradesh

Lok Raj Party Himachal Pradesh (People's Rule Party Himachal Pradesh) was a political party in the Indian state of Himachal Pradesh in the beginning of the 1970's. LRP was led by Thakur Sen Negi, formely leader of the Samyukt Vidhayak Dal in the state. Another important leader was the former Congress leader J.B.L. Khachi.

LRP contested the 1971 Lok Sabha elections and the 1972 state assembly elections.

In the 1972 state assembly elections LRP had put up candidates in 16 out of 68 constituencies. Two were elected. In total the party received 44067 votes (5,02% of the votes in the state).

Loktantrik Morcha (Himachal Pradesh)

Loktantrik Morcha (Himachal Pradesh) (Democratic Front (Himachal Pradesh)), a political party in the Indian state of Himachal Pradesh. LM (HP) was registered as a political party in 2003. It is led by Mohinder Singh Chaudhury, former Himachal Vikas Congress minister and convenor of Him Loktantrik Morcha.

Singh had been Public Works Department Minister in the HVC-BJP cabinet in the state. But shortly after the 1998 elections, a group of BJP legislators demanded his resignation on ground of corruption. HVC leader Sukh Ram had to bow to their demand, and Singh was expelled from HVC. Initially Singh joined Lok Janshakti Party. Ahead of the 2003 assembly elections he launched LM(HP) as a political party and was elected as its sole member of the assembly. In total LM(HP) had 14 candidates, who together got 66102 votes (2,17% of the votes in the state).

In the 2004 elections LM(HP) supported the BJP-led National Democratic Alliance. Ahead of the elections there were discussions on a merger with BJP, but most probably the electoral defeat of BJP had stopped that process.

4

Language and Literature

LANGUAGES OF HIMACHAL PRADESH

The people of the state of Himachal Pradesh are multilingual and converse in several languages. The official state language of Himachal Pradesh is Hindi. The other most popular language of Himachal Pradesh is Pahari. Other than these Punjabi, Dogri, Kangri and Kinnauri language is also used in Himachal Pradesh.

Hindi is declared as the official state language of Himachal Pradesh. The language of Hindi is an old derivative of the Sanskrit language. It is spoken in the country in several dialects. Hindi language is also used in the state of Himachal Pradesh as a mode of interaction among people. The government has inculcated the study of Hindi in the academic curriculum and also encourages the use of the language in professional spectrum. The people of the state prevalently use the Pahari language. The Pahari language is derived from the ancient language of Sanskrit and Prakrit. The language is divided into three forms. These are Northern Pahari, Eastern Pahari and Western Pahari. The Western Pahari form is predominantly used in the state of Himachal Pradesh. The Pahari dialects of Sirmauri and Keonthali are spoken in the region of Simla. Some of the other

Pahari dialects spoken in Himachal Pradesh are Chambiali, Churahi, Mandeali, Himachali and Kuluhi.

The use of language in Himachal Pradesh depends also on the various communities that have settled in the hilly terrain. The different communities use other languages to communicate as well. The use of Punjabi language is popular. The languages Dogri, Kangri and Kinnauri are prevalently used by the local people of the state.

Languages of Himachal Pradesh (2011)

Hindi (85.88%)

Punjabi (8.96%)

Nepali (1.30%)

Kashmiri (0.83%)

Others (3.03%)

Hindi is the official language of Himachal Pradesh and is spoken by the majority of the population as a lingua franca. English is given the status of an additional official language. Most of the languages spoken natively belong to the group of the Himachali languages. According to the 2001 Census of India, the languages spoken in the state in descending order of native speakers are Hindi, spoken by 89.01% of the population (including Himachali languages as dialects of Hindi); followed by Punjabi (5.99%), Nepali (1.16%) and Kinnauri (1.06%).

LANGUAGE SPOKEN

Himachal Pradesh is one of the Indian States where the people are capable of speaking many languages. Though the official language of Himachal Pradesh is Hindi, majority of the people also speak well in pahari. They also converse in Punjabi, Kangri, Kinnauri and Dogri.

The state's official language is Hindi, which is a very ancient language that gained its origin from Sanskrit. Hindi is being used in various dialects throughout the country. In Himachal Pradesh, this language is used as a means of communication between populates. In order to improve the significance of the language, the government has included Hindi in the educational curriculum. Apart from this, they also encourage the language to be used professionally. Generally, majority of the people of Himachal Pradesh converse in Pahari language, the origin of which is from the oldest language Pakrit and Sanskrit.

The Pahari language is mainly subdivided into three types; the Eastern Pahari, Western Pahari and the Northern Pahari. In Himachal Pradesh, western Pahari is the most commonly used language, while in its capital city Simla, the dialects of Keonthali and Sirmauri are used. Himachali, Kuluhi, Chambiali, Churahi and Mandeali are some of the other various dialects of Pahari language.

The different communities that are being settled down in the mountainous terrain determine the language that is used in the state of Himachal Pradesh. Various other languages are also used by diverse communities for their communication. One of the most popular languages of this state is Punjabi and languages like Kangri and Kinnauri are also used by the local residents.

As stated earlier, Pahari is the language used by the majority of the people and it is derived from Sanskrit, the oldest language of India. Most of the basic words of Pahari are from Sanskrit and Pakrit is the other language from which several words are taken by Pahari.

Apart from these languages, Himachal Pradesh is flourished with several tribal languages, since numerous varied types of tribes are settled in this state. Being a big state, the language used by the people varies with every region. Some of the regional languages that are spoken in this state are Chambyali, Pangwali, Lahauli and Kinnauri.

Hindi

Hindi is not only the official language of Himachal Pradesh but also for India. Though being derived from Sanskrit, Hindi is widely spoken throughout the country and ranks third among the most common spoken languages all over the world.

Punjabi language

Punjabi is an Indo-Aryan language which is widely used by the Punjabi community living in India and Pakistan and all through the world. This language is also used in Himachal Pradesh along with the various other languages. This is mainly because of the tribes who speak Punjabi language settled in the western and central parts of Himachal Pradesh.

Pahari language

Pahar language is widely used by the people of North India who are residing in hilly areas. There are various forms of dialect available for this language. The Pahari language or as they are popularly called the Pahari languages is a cluster of identical dialects which are used by the people living near the Himalayan foothills and the North Indians. Even people of Nepal use this language. Apart from the main divisions of Pahari language, eastern, western and Central Pahari, Garhwali is another classification. Some of the languages that come under Garhwali are Gaddi and Dogri.

Though various languages are being spoken in Himachal Pradesh, all are closely similar with minute variations among them.

5

Geography and Flora & Fauna

GEOGRAPHY OF HIMACHAL PRADESH

View of Reo Purgyil, second highest peak in Himachal Pradesh

The state of Himachal Pradesh is spread over an area 55,673 km² and is bordered by Jammu and Kashmir on the north, Punjab on the southwest, Haryana on the south, Uttarakhand on the southeast and Tibet on the east. Himachal is a mountainous region, rich in its natural resources.

Characteristics

Elevation ranges from 450 metres to over 7,026(Shilla Peak) metres above sea level. The region extends from the Shivalik range of mountains (barely mountainous region). There is a noticeable increase in elevation from west to east and from south to north. At 7026 m Shilla is the highest mountain peak in the state of Himachal Pradesh.

The general physiographic divisions from south to north are:

1. The outer Himalayas (Shivaliks)
2. The lesser Himalayas (central zone)
3. The Great Himalayas (northern zone)
4. Zanskar range (shilla Peak-kinnaur, Pangi chamba).

The Shiwalik range consists of lower hills (600 m above sea level). The hills of the region are composed of highly unconsolidated deposits which results in a high rate of erosion and deforestation.

The lesser Himalayas are spotted by a gradual elevation towards the Dhauladhar and the Pir Panjal ranges. The rise is more rapid in the Shimla hills, to the south of which is the high peak of church — Chandni (3647 m). North of the river Sutlej, the rise is steady.

The Kangra valley is a longitudinal trough which is at the foot of the Dhauladhar range. Dhauladhar (which means the 'White Peak') has a mean elevation of nearly 4,550 metres. It has a rapid rise of 3,600 m above the Kangra valley. The largest of the lesser Himalayan ranges, the Pir Panjal, branches off from the Greater Himalayan range near the bank of the Sutlej. A number of glaciers exist and several passes lie across the Pir Panjal. The Rohtang Pass (3,978 m) is one of these.

The Great Himalayan range (5,000 to 6,000 metres) runs along the eastern boundary and is slashed across by the Sutlej. Some of the famous passes in this range are Kangla (5,248 m),

Bara Lacha (4,512 m), Parang (5,548 m) and Pin Parvati (4,802 m).

The Zaskar Range, the easternmost range, separates Kinnaur and Spiti from Tibet. It has peaks up to 7,026 m high. Some of the well-known peaks are Shilla(7,026 m) and Riwo Phargyul (6,791 m); these are among the highest peaks in this range. There are many glaciers over the Zaskar and the Great Himalayan ranges.

Himachal is well known for its rich flora. Forests cover about 38% of the state's area. It has a variety of wildlife, too.

Himachal has 49 cities and towns. The smallest town is Naina Devi and the largest is Shimla with a total state population of 6,856,509. Urban population is only 7.5% of the state population. Most of the population resides in rural areas.

CLIMATE OF HIMACHAL PRADESH

There is a huge variation in the climatic conditions of Himachal Pradesh due to variation in altitude (450–6500 metres). The climate varies from hot and sub-humid tropical (450–900 metres) in the southern low tracts, warm and temperate (900–1800 metres), cool and temperate (1900–2400 metres) and cold glacial and alpine (2400–4800 metres) in the northern and eastern high elevated mountain ranges.

By October, nights and mornings are very cold. Snowfall at elevations of nearly 3000 m is about 3 m and lasts from December start to March end. About 4500 m, is perpetual snow.

The spring season starts from mid February to mid April. The weather is pleasant and comfortable in the season.

The rainy season start at the end of the month of June. The landscape lushes green and fresh. During the season streams and natural springs are replenished. The heavy rains in July and August cause a lot of damage resulting in erosion, floods and landslides. Out of all the state districts, Dharamsala receives the highest rainfall, nearly about 3400 mm. Spiti is the driest area of the state (rainfall below 50mm). The reason is that it is enclosed by high mountains on all sides.

GEOGRAPHY AND CLIMATE

Himachal is in the western Himalayas. Covering an area of 55,673 square kilometres (21,495 sq mi), it is a mountainous state. Most of the state lies on the foothills of the Dhauladhar Range. At 6,816 m Reo Purgyil is the highest mountain peak in the state of Himachal Pradesh.

The drainage system of Himachal is composed both of rivers and glaciers. Himalayan rivers criss-cross the entire mountain chain. Himachal Pradesh provides water to both the Indus and Ganges basins. The drainage systems of the region are the Chandra Bhaga or the Chenab, the Ravi, the Beas, the Sutlej, and the Yamuna. These rivers are perennial and are fed by snow and rainfall. They are protected by an extensive cover of natural vegetation.

Due to extreme variation in elevation, great variation occurs in the climatic conditions of Himachal. The climate varies from hot and subhumid tropical in the southern tracts to, with more elevation, cold, alpine, and glacial in the northern and eastern mountain ranges. The state's winter capital, Dharamsala receives very heavy rainfall, while areas like Lahaul and Spiti are cold and almost rainless. Broadly, Himachal experiences three seasons: summer, winter, and rainy season. Summer lasts from mid-April till the end of June and most parts become very hot (except in the alpine zone which experiences a mild summer) with the average temperature ranging from 28 to 32 °C (82 to 90 °F). Winter lasts from late November till mid March. Snowfall is common in alpine tracts (generally above 2,200 metres (7,218 ft) i.e. in the higher and trans-Himalayan region).

GEOGRAPHY AND CLIMATE

Districts

- Kangra
- Hamirpur
- Mandi

- Bilaspur
- Una
- Chamba
- Lahul and Spiti
- Sirmaur
- Kinnaur
- Kullu
- Solan
- Shimla, Shimla city, the state's capital is part of this district.

LOCATION

Himachal Pradesh ("Snowy Mountain State") is located in the extreme northwest of India, almost at the extremity of the large, densely populated part of Asia influenced by the southwest monsoon. It has a long border with Jammu, Kashmir and Ladakh on the northwestern side and in the northern districts of Spiti and Kinnaur, there is a border with China (Tibet). All these borders, except in the extreme southwest where there is a major road to Jammu town, are formed by extremely high passes that are snowbound except between mid-July and mid-October. To the east is the state of Uttarakhand (formerly part of Uttar Pradesh), the border with which is, apart from the southern section which is virtually part of the Indo-Gangetic Plain, even less accessible than those to the north. There is a road to that states provisional capital Dehra Dun from Nahan in the extreme south of the state.

To the south Himachal Pradesh is bordered by the states of Punjab, Haryana and Uttar Pradesh from east to west. Most of the area near the borders is easily accessible and flat-Chandigarh is only about 25 kilometres (15.5 miles) by road from the Himachal border.

CLIMATE

There is great diversification in the climatic conditions of Himachal due to variation in elevation (450-6500 mtrs). It varies from hot and sub-humid tropical (450-900 mtrs) in the southern Low tracts, warm and temperate (900-1800 mtrs), cool and temperate (1900-2400 mtrs) and cold alpine and glacial (2400-4800 mtrs) in the northern and eastern high mountain ranges.

The year is divided into three seasons. Cold (October to February), hot (March to June) and rainy (July to September). By October, nights and mornings are very cold.

Snowfall at elevations of about 3000 mtrs is about 3 mtrs and lasts from December to March. About 4500 mtrs, is perpetual snow.

The main season is the spring from mid-Feb to March-April. The air is cool and fresh. Colourful flowers adorn the valleys, forest slopes and meadows. In the hill stations, the climate is pleasant and comfortable.

The rains start at the end of June. The entire landscape becomes green and fresh. Streams begin to swell and springs are replenished. The heavy rains in July and August cause damage to erosion, floods and landslides.

Dharamsala has the highest rainfall of 3400 mm. Spiti is the driest area (below 50 mm rainfall) being enclosed by high mountains on all sides.

RIVERS

Himachal provides water to both the Indus and Ganges basins. The major river systems of the region are the Chandrabhaga or the Chenab, the Ravi, the Beas, the Sutlej and the Yamuna. These perennial rivers are fed by snow and rainfall and are protected by a fairly extensive cover of natural vegetation.

The Beas (Vedic name Arjikiya and in later Sanskrit Vipasa) rises in the Pir Panjal range near the Rohtang Pass and flows some 256 km in Himachal. The river is formed by a number of tributaries, the important being the Parbati, the Hurla, the Sainj, the Uhl, the Suheti, the Luni, the Banganga and the Chaki.

The northern and eastern tributaries of the Beas are snow fed and perennial, while the southern affluent are seasonal. During August, increase in inflow sometimes results in floods. It passes through Kullu and Manali districts and enters Kangra.

The 435 feet Pong Dam is constructed on the Beas River just before Talwara in Punjab. The Pong Dam wetland is the site of a famous bird sanctuary and over 220 species of bird have been recorded here.

The Chandrabhaga or Chenab (Vedic name Askni), the largest river (in terms of volume of water) is formed by the confluence of 2 streams, the Chandra and the Bhaga at Tundi, in Lahaul. It flows 122 km and has a catchments area of 7500 km^2 in Himachal. It passes through the Lahaul valley, enters Kashmir near Kishtwar and eventually reaches Pakistan.

The Ravi (Vedic name Purushni and in later Sanskrit Iravati) is born in Bara Banghal, Kangra district as a joint stream formed by the glacier fed Bhadal and Tantgari. The river has a length of about 158 km and has a catchment area of about 5451 km. The Chamba district lies on its right Bank.

The Sutlej (Vedic name Saturdi and in later Sanskrit Shatadru) originates in distant Tibet. It cuts through both the great Himalayan and the Zanskar ranges and crosses the Indo-Tibetan border near Shipkila. River Spiti then joins it from the north. Passing through precipitous gorges and narrow valleys it emerges from the mountains at Bhakra near the Nangal town in Punjab.

The catchment area of Sutlej in Himachal is 20,000 km^2. The Bhakra Nangal Dam is constructed on river Sutlej. The reservoir created by the dam is called "Gobind Sagar" and covers nearly 170 km^2. The reservoir is an important water sports site in Himachal and a major fishing resource. The bridge on the Sutlej River at Kandraur, Bilaspur District is one of the highest in Asia.

The Yamuna originates from Yamunotri glacier near the Bandar Punch Peak in Uttar Kashi district of Uttarakhand. It is also fed by the Champasar glaciers. Its total catchment area in Himachal is 2320 km^2.

Its main tributaries are the Tons, the Giri and the Bata. It passes through Paunta Sahib in the Sirmaur district of Himachal.

FLORA AND FAUNA OF HIMACHAL PRADESH

Himachal is a land of jade forests and fresh air. As much as 68% of the land area is covered with jungles. While the foothills and valleys are a refreshing green, the areas above the snow line are almost bare.

The southernmost tracts are dominated by sal (Shorea robusta), sisham, chir pine, dry deciduous and moist broad-leafed forests. The temperate region above this grows oaks, deodar, blue pine, fir and spruce. In the uppermost climes, trees are sturdy with a vast network of roots (to help them tide over the weeks of burial under heavy snow). You'll mostly find alders, birches, rhododendrons and moist alpine scrubs in the name of vegetation. The tough rhododendron, by the way, is an amazing plant and of terrific importance in the ecological chain. By attracting insects, which in turn attract birds, it forms a major link in high altitude ecosystems. The rhododendrons you see along the hillsides around Shimla from March to May are breathtakingly beautiful.

Himachal is the fruit bowl of the country with orchards scattered all over the place. Meadows and pastures are often seen clinging to the dangerously steep slopes. After the winter snow thaws, the hillsides and orchards bloom with wild flowers, while gladiolas, carnations, marigolds, roses, chrysanthemums, tulips, lilies and other flowers are carefully cultivated. The state government is gearing up to make Himachal the flower basket of the world.

From thick sub-tropical forests to the dry alpine vegetation, Himachal home to a wide variety of animals. This includes the leopard, which is the most widely distributed mammal in the entire state, the snow leopard, ghoral (goat-like stout animal), musk deer which is the state animal and monal (a pretty bird in nine iridescent colours), the state bird. HP has 11 major national parks and sanctuaries – the largest number in the Himalayan region. The Great Himalayan National Park in Kullu – the first in the state – was created to conserve the flora and fauna of the main Himalayan range, while the Pin Valley National Park to conserve the flora and fauna of the cold desert.

Flora and fauna

Asian paradise flycatcher in Kullu

Himachal Pradesh is one of the states that lies in the Indian Himalayan Region (IHR), one of the richest reservoirs of biological diversity in the world. The IHR is currently undergoing large scale irrational extraction of wild, medicinal herbs, thus endangering many of its high-value gene stock. To address this, a workshop on 'Endangered Medicinal Plant Species in Himachal Pradesh' was held in 2002 and the conference was attended by forty experts from diverse disciplines.

Black Bulbul (Hypsipetes leucocephalus). Solan (Himachal Pradesh). 28-July-2013

According to 2003 Forest Survey of India report, legally defined forest areas constitute 66.52% of the area of Himachal Pradesh. Vegetation in the state is dictated by elevation and precipitation. The state endows with a high diversity of medicinal and aromatic plants. Lahaul-Spiti region of the state, being a cold desert, supports unique plants of medicinal value including *Ferula jaeschkeana*, *Hyoscyamus niger*, *Lancea tibetica*, and *Saussurea bracteata*.

Himachal is also said to be the fruit bowl of the country, with orchards being widespread. Meadows and pastures are also seen clinging to steep slopes. After the winter season, the hillsides and orchards bloom with wild flowers, while gladiolas, carnations, marigolds, roses, chrysanthemums, tulips and lilies are carefully cultivated. Himachal Pradesh Horticultural Produce Marketing and Processing Corporation Ltd. (HPMC) is a state body that markets fresh and processed fruits.

Himachal Pradesh has around 463 bird 77 mammalian, 44

reptile and 80 fish species. Great Himalayan National Park, a UNESCO World Heritage Site and Pin Valley National Park are the national Parks located in the state. The state also has 30 wildlife sanctuariesand 3 conservation reserves.

Incredible Himachal

Himachal Pradesh also called Himachal, is an Indian state located along the northern part of country at the foot of lower Himalayas. Himachal Pradesh shares its borders with other Indian states like Jammu and Kashmir, Punjab, Haryana, and Uttarakhand.

It also shares international border with Tibet. Himachal Pradesh's total area is approximately 55,000 square kilometers. The presence of varied landscape like hills, valleys, lush meadows, peaks, forests, lakes, rivers and fertile lands make this state a favorite destination for tourists.

The most prominent river of the state is Sutlej and Beas. The high altitude topography and cold climate conditions of the state is house for numerous, unique flora and fauna. Majority of these are among categories of rarest and exclusively found in the hill state alone.

The Himalayas play a vital role in deciding excellent quality of life in India. The presence of varied geographical location which is usually found in a continent are found in India and this has earned the name of sub continent for the country. The presence of Himalayas has contributed to diversified climatic and geographical conditions. It has largely affected the life of people and their living style etc. Also, this diversified geographical location has proved to be a rich source of natural resources no matter they are living and hidden.

The variations in altitude have given rise to varied vegetation and this has emerged as the house for numerous varieties of birds as well as animals. The flora of Himalayas is very distinctive as it consists of diverse forests. It consists of forests of all types like hot and cold deserts, alpine meadows, rhododendron forests, coniferous forests, deciduous forests and tropical swampy forests. The state is not only a dwelling point for human habitat and birth place of human civilization, but also the abode of numerous plant and animal species. Himalayas are the youngest mountain ranges in the world, which is full of treasure of flora and fauna. The geological structure of Himalayas is not stabilized and this makes its ecosystem to remain weak.

The Variation of Elevation in Himachal and Its Effects

The highest regions of the state fall in eastern and northern area, those situated on the foot of Himalayas. The elevation of these areas is in the range of 4,500 to 7,000 meters above sea level. The important mountain in this range is Zanskar Mountains (near Spiti which has peaks of an altitude of over 6500 meters), the Shilla peak (stands tall at 7,000 meters) and Riwo Phargyul summit (located at an altitude of more than 6,800 meters above sea level).

These high elevation areas also have several famous passes. The prominent ones are Kangra pass (placed at around 5,200 meters), Bara Lacha pass (approximately 4,500 meters), and Pin Parbati pass (located at 4,800 meters above sea level). These high altitude areas also contain several glaciers and forests.

The state of Himachal also has some regions which form part of lower Himalayas whose altitude varies somewhere between 1000 meters to 4500 meters above sea level. The lower Himalayan region is the abode for numerous mountain ranges like Dhauladhar range, Pir Panjal range and Shimla hills. The Dhauladhar range, which forms part of Kangra valley, is famous for its excellent landscape and picturesque locations. They are placed at an altitude of more than 4500 meters above sea level. The Pir Panjal range, adjoining Satluj river bank houses several glaciers and a good number of passes. The most prominent among these passes is Rohtang Pass, located above 4,000 meters from sea level and connects Leh with the state. The southern

Shimla hill is popular due to the presence of Chandni peak stands tall at 3,600 meters above sea level.

The state also houses a small mountain range called Shivalik Mountains. These are also called as Outer Himalayas and contain certain hills of altitude ranges of 1000 meters above sea level.

Full of Flora and Fauna

The survey conducted by Forest Department of India defines total forest area of the state to be 66.52%. However, the total area covered by trees includes just 25.78%. The complete vegetation of this region relies on two factors - height and rainfall. The southernmost part of the state is at a lower altitude level and it contains both humid and subtropical dry broadleaf woodlands, along with subtropical moist broadleaf forests. The majority of area is covered by Himalayan subtropical broadleaf forests. Apart from this we also have some of the vegetation which is abundant with sal, sisham, chir pine, dry deciduous and moist broad-leafed forests. The landscape which falls in temperate regions has some of the prominent trees like oaks, deodar, blue pine, fir and spruce. The places that lie in top elevation have numerous trees that are sturdy and contain roots that run deep into the earth. Some of the commonly found trees in these regions include Alders, birches, rhododendrons and moist alpine scrubs. The rhododendron is a common type of tree in the Shimla region and this is seen in abundance in months between March to May.

Himachal has abundant growth of fruits like apple, peaches, plums and berries. It is rightly called the 'fruit bowl of India'. There are plenty of fruit orchards and fruits are exported to various parts of the country and abroad. Lush Meadows and paddock can be seen along hillocks and steep lying areas. Post winter season the hilly regions and orchards are full of fruits. The pleasant climate helps numerous flower varieties like gladiolas, lilies, tulips, chrysanthemums, roses, marigolds, carnations etc to grow in abundance. The state government is dedicated in making the state 'the flower basket of the world' and for this there has been good initiative from all corners towards this commitment.

The state is house for numerous species of habitat. The state is the resting place for approximately 1200 birds along with 359 animal species. Some of the animals which form members of this vast list are leopards, ghoral, snow leopard, musk deer (state animal) and Western Tragopan (state bird). The state is an ideal tourist destination for animal lovers as it hosts 12 main national parks & sanctuaries. The state also has the distinction of hosting maximum number of sanctuaries in Himalayan region. The Kullu district hosts The Great Himalayan National Park, which was established with the main aim to protect endangered fauna and flora of main Himalayan Mountains. Similarly Pin Valley National Park conserves the flora and fauna of popular cold desert.

Ideal Time to Visit

Plan your trip during the months of January to April to enjoy the nature's beauty at its best and abundant flora and fauna.

6

Economy

ECONOMY OF HIMACHAL PRADESH

The era of economic planning started in Himachal Pradesh in 1948. The first five-year plan allocated about Rs. 52.7 million to Himachal. More than 50% of this expenditure was spent on transport facilities since it was felt that without proper it, the process of planning and development couldn't be carried.

The community development programme which was launched in 1952 in Himachal, in certain selected areas was later extended to the entire rural Himachal. In Mandi and Kangra, package programmes were undertaken in collaboration with the West Germany for popularising modern techniques of cultivation among the farmers. Suitable agricultural machinery and animal husbandry were introduced in these areas. Well equipped soil testing laboratories, dairy farms and agricultural workshops were set up at various centres, besides an Agriculture University at Palampur.

Himachal is one of those states in India which was rapidly transformed from the most backward part of the country to one of the most advanced states. At present Himachal ranks fourth in respect of per capita income among the states of the Indian Union.

Himachal education system is well established, its agriculture is enough for its self-sufficiency, its horticulture is highly impressive in the country and even in abroad, its road connectivity system has emerged as the best in the mountainous areas in India, the infrastructure for its industrial development are well laid out, its rich forest resources being augmented and above all, the increasing attention of the nation towards the exploitation of its hydel resources are the signs for its bright future.

It has already become the ideal in respect of development for the hill areas of the country.

Shimla, the capital of Himachal Pradesh. Shimla Montage - Clockwise from top: Skyline at Shimla Southern Side, Indian Institute of Advanced Studies formerly(Viceregal Lodge, Rashtrapati Niwas), Town hall, Night view of Shimla and Christ Church.

Gross State Domestic Product at Current Prices

figures in crores of Indian Rupees

Year	Gross State Domestic Product
1980	794
1985	1,372
1990	2,815
1995	6,698
2000	13,590
2005	23,024
2006	25,435
2010	57,452
2013	82,585
2014	92,589
2015	101,108

2016	110,511
2017	124,570
2018	135,914

The era of planning in Himachal Pradesh started in 1951 along with the rest of India with the implementation of the first five-year plan. The First Plan allocated 52.7 million to Himachal Pradesh. More than 50% of this expenditure was incurred on transport and communication; while the power sector got a share of just 4.6%, though it had steadily increased to 7% by the Third Plan. Expenditure on agriculture and allied activities increased from 14.4% in the First Plan to 32% in the Third Plan, showing a progressive decline afterwards from 24% in the Fourth Plan to less than 10% in the Tenth Plan.Expenditure on energy sector was 24.2% of the total in the Tenth Plan. The total GDP for 2005-06 was estimated at 254 billion as against 230 billion in the year 2004–05, showing an increase of 10.5%. The GDP for fiscal 2015-16 was estimated at 1.110 trillion recording an annual growth of 7.7%. As per the advance estimates for fiscal 2016-17, the state's GDP increased to 1.247 trillion. The per capita incomes for fiscal years 2015-16 and 2016-17 were estimated at 130,067 and 147,277 respectively. The state government's advance estimates for fiscal 2017-18 stated the total GDP and per capita income as 1.359 trillion and 158,462 respectively. Himachal now ranks one of the highest among the states and union territories of India in terms of per capita income.

Himachal Pradesh also ranks as the second best performing state in the country on human development indicators after Kerala. One of the Indian government's key initiatives to tackle unemployment is the National Rural Employment Guarantee Act (NREGA). The participation of women in the NREGA has been observed to vary across different regions of the nation. As of the year 2009-2010, Himachal Pradesh joined the category of high female participation, recording a 46% share of NREGS (National Rural Employment Guarantee Scheme) work days to women. This was a drastic increase from the 13% that was recorded in 2006-2007.

AGRICULTURE

Himalayas from Kullu Valley

Agriculture contributes about 9.4% to the net state domestic product. It is the main source of income and employment in Himachal. About 90% of the population in Himachal depends directly upon agriculture, which provides direct employment to 62% of total workers of state. The main cereals grown include wheat, maize, rice and barley with major cropping systems being maize-wheat, rice-wheat and maize-potato-wheat. Pulses, fruits, vegetables and oilseeds are among the other crops grown in the state. Land husbandry initiatives such as the Mid-Himalayan Watershed Development Project, which includes the Himachal Pradesh Reforestation Project (HPRP), the world's largest clean development mechanism (CDM) undertaking, have improved agricultural yields and productivity, and raised rural household incomes.

Apple is the principal cash crop of the state grown principally in the districts of Shimla, Kinnaur, Kullu, Mandi, Chamba and some parts of Sirmaur and Lahaul-Spiti with an average annual production of 5 lakh tonnes and per hectare production of 8 to 10 tonnes. The apple cultivation constitute 49 per cent of the total area under fruit crops and 85% of total fruit production in the state with an estimated economy of 3500 crore. Apples from Himachal are exported to other Indian states and even other countries. In 2011-12, the total area under apple cultivation was 1.04 lakh hectares, increased from 90,347 hectares in 2000-01. According to the provisional estimates of Ministry of Agriculture & Farmers Welfare, the annual apple production in Himachal for fiscal 2015-16 stood at 7.53 lakh tonnes, making it India's second largest apple producing state after Jammu and Kashmir.

Energy

Hydropower is also one of the major sources of income generation for the state. The state has an abundance of hydropower resources because of the presence of various perennial rivers. Many high capacity projects are being constructed to capitalize on these. In addition, the rich hydropower resources of Himachal have resulted in the state becoming almost universally electrified with around 94.8% houses receiving electricity as of 2001, as compared to the national average of 55.9%. The income generated from exporting the electricity to other states is being provided as subsidy to the consumers in the state. Himachal's hydro-electric power production is however yet to be fully utilized. The identified Hydroelectric Potential for the state is 27,436 MW in five river basins and the annual hydroelectricity production in 2016 was 10,351 MW.

Agriculture

Agriculture contributes nearly about 45% to the net state domestic product. It is the main source of income as well as employment in Himachal. About 93% of the state population depend directly upon agriculture. The main cereals grown in the state are wheat, maize, rice and barley. Kangra, Mandi and Paonta valley of Sirmaur district (to some extent) are the major producers of the first three cereals, while barley is mostly cultivated in Shimla. Fruit cultivation has also proved to be an economic boon to the state.

There are huge tracts of land suitable only for growing fruits. Fruit of all cultivation does not add to the problem of soil erosion and its employment potential is more than the conventional farming. The yield per acre in terms of income is also much higher.

Apple produces the maximum income. Fruit growing in the state is fetching over Rs. 3 billion annually. Special efforts are being made to promote cultivation of crops like olives, figs, hops, mushrooms, flowers, pistachio nuts, sarda melon and saffron. The state has also earned the name of the *Apple State of India.*

POWER

Himachal Pradesh is extremely rich in its hydel resources. The state is having about twenty five percent of the national potential in this aspect.

It has been estimated that about 20,300 MW of hydel power can be generated in the state by the construction of various hydel projects on the five river basins no matter they are major medium or small.

The state government has been giving the highest priority for its development, since hydel generation can meet the growing need of power for industry, agriculture and rural electrification. It is also the biggest source of income to the state as it provides electricity to the other states also.

One of the major project on river Sutlej in the state is the *Nathpa Jhakri* which generates nearly 1500MW of electricity. The following project is funded by World Bank.

MAJOR ONGOING PROJECTS

- Chamera II Hydel Project in June 1999-300MW
- Parbati Hydel Power Project in December 1999,-2051MW
- Kol Dam project in June 2000-800MW

- Bhaba Augmentation Scheme, Ghanvi Hydro Electric Project-22.5MW
- Larji Hydel Project-126MW
- Khauli Hydro Electric Project-12MW
- The state government has given eight hydel projects for private sector participation. Some of these are:
  - o Baspa Hydro Electric Project-300MW
  - o Holi Hydro Electric Project-231MW
  - o Dhamwari Sunda Hydro Electric Project-70MW
  - o Allian Duhangan Hydro Electric Project-192MW
  - o Swara-Kuddu-162MW
  - o Budhil-70MW

PROTECTED AREAS

Forest in Himachal Pradesh cover an area of nearly 21,325 sq. km. that is about 38.3% of the total area of the state. The state government aims to provide green cover to 50% of the total area. Earlier forests were considered to be the main source of income of the state. Now the stress has been from shifted from exploitation to conservation. Forests have been completely nationalized under the supervision of Indian forest service.

Reckless cutting of trees and sale of timber is now conducted by the State Forest Corporation. A World Bank assisted *Social Forestry Project* has been launched. The project aims at raising fuel, fodder and timber species to meet the basic requirements of the people so that it do not lead to the depletion of forests. An *Enforcement Organisation* has been established to keep a check on the illegal cutting of trees and smuggling of timber.

An integrated *water shed department* project for Shivaliks is under construction. Another project for the afforestation of barren *Kandi* areas has also been undertaken with the cooperation of the World Bank. Steps are also been taken to intensify preservation and management. Hunting has also been restricted. At present there are 32 Sanctuaries, 2 National parks and 3 Games Reserves.

Fact and Figures

Forest Cover (1996-1997)	*Area*
Reserved Forests	1896 sq.kms.
Protected Forests	43043 sq.kms.
Unclassed Forest	976 sq.kms.
Other Forests	370 sq.kms.
Forests not under control of forest Deptt.	748 sq.kms.

Sancturies and National Parks

Sanctuaries and National Parks	*Area (km^2)*	*Year of Notification*
Simbalbara Sanctuary	17.20	1958
Great Himalayan National Park	605.61	1984
Pin Valley National Park	807.36	1987
Kanwar Sanctuary	61.57	1954
Kalatop Khajjiar Sanctuary	30.69	1949
Renuka Sanctuary	7.02	1957
Manali Sanctuary	31.27	1954
Churdhar Sanctuary	56.59	1985
Maharana Pratap Sagar Sanctuary	322.70	1983
Daranghati Sanctuary	27.01	1962
Chail Sanctuary	110.04	1976
Majthal Sanctuary	31.64	1962

HYDROELECTRIC POWER IN HIMACHAL PRADESH

Himachal Pradesh is extremely rich in its hydroelectricity resources. The state is having about twenty five percent of the national potential in this aspect. It has been estimated that about 27,436 MW of hydel power can be generated in the state by the construction of various hydel projects on the five perennial river basins no matter they are major, medium or small. Out of total hydel potential of the state, 8,418 MW is harnessed so far, out of which only 7.6% is under the control of Himachal Pradesh Government while the rest being exploited by the Central Government. The state government has been giving the highest priority for its development, since hydel generation can meet the growing need of power for industry, agriculture and rural electrification. It is also the biggest source of income to the state as it provides electricity to the other states also.

Himachal has enough resources to generate surplus power but, sometimes this is a misconception as in winters the power shortage overshoots ten lakh units per day due to less flow of water in rivers and at the same time increase in lighting and heating load. Due to increased industrialization and rural electrification this figure is expected to rise even further.

Completed projects

Girinagar Hydel Project

Situated on the river *Giri* of the Sirmour District, Girinagar Hydel project has an installed capacity of 60MW, with 2 units of 30MW each. This project, which is run-off-the-river scheme comes under HPSEB and is operational for 29 years.121

Binwa Hydel Project

The project with an installed capacity office 16MW comprising 3 units each, is located near Baijnath in District Kangra. The project is situated 25 km from Palampur and 14 km from Baijnath is constructed at an elevation of 1515 mets. above the mean sea level. This project constitutes a 62 mets. long tunnel that connects trench weirs in Banu Khad and Prahal Khud.

Sanjay Vidyut Pariyojna

Located in the Kinnaur district, on the river Bhaba is a completely underground project with an installed capacity of

120MW, comprising 3 units each of 40MW. The uniqueness of this project lies in its underground switchyard, a feature that no other hydel project in Asia can brag about. Completed in 1989-90, the estimated cost was about 167 crore rupees. The total length of tunnels including those secured in after completing the project is 12 km.

Bassi Hydroelectric Project

Bassi project(66MW) is an extension of Beas Power House (Mandi District) constituting 4 units of 16.5MW each. It utilizes the tail water of Shanon Power House of Joginder Nagar project and generates 145MW per annum.

Larji Hydroelectric Project

Larji hydroelectric project is on river Beas in Kullu district with an installed capacity of 126 MW. The project was completed in September 2007.

Andhra Hydel Project

Commissioned during the year 1987-88, the project has 3 units of 5.5MW which makes it 16.5MW of installed capacity. It is located in Rohru tehsil of Shimla district. The cost of the project was estimated to be around 9.74 crores, generating 89MW per annum and it transmitting to the state grid via the Neogli power house near Rampur.

Rongtong Hydel Project

Rongtong is a 2MW project that is located in the *Lahaul-Spiti district* on Rongtong Nullaha, a tributary of *Spiti* river. Located at an elevation of 3,600 metres in a snow adhered region, this was the first hydel project executed for the socio-economic upliftment of the tribals of this area. It is one of the highest in the world. The snow fed water runnel tapped at an elevation of 3,788 mets. is diverted through 2,825 mets. long channel and 259 mets. long tunnel into an open reservoir with a capacity of 14,000 cubic mets. Renovated by APE Power Pvt. Ltd., APE Power also renovate RUKTI (4 x 375 KW) Hydro Electric project.

Baner and Neugal Project

With the combined installed capacity of 12MW the projects are situated on Baner and Neugal streams respectively in Kangra District. Both of the streams emerge from Dhauladhar and join Beas in the form of tributaries in south.

Nathpa Jhakri Project

One of the major project on the Sutlej river is the *Nathpa Jhakri Dam* which generates nearly 1500MW of electricity. The project is funded by World Bank. its construction cost is around 8000 crores

Sainj Hydroelectric Project

Installed Capacity 100MW. [50MW*2Units]

Bhakra Dam

The Bhakra Dam has the first Dam to have come up on the Satluj river, it is one of the highest gravity dams in the world and has an Installed capacity of 1325 MW. The dam holds excess waters during the monsoon and provides a regulated release during the year . It also prevents damage due to monsoon floods. The dam provides irrigation to 10 million acres (40,000 km^2) of fields in Punjab, Haryana, and Rajasthan.

TRANSPORT IN HIMACHAL PRADESH

The development of tribal areas in Himachal Pradesh is one of the major steps taken by the state government for its economic development.

The border districts of Kinnaur, Lahaul, Spiti and the *Pangi* and *Bharmour* tehsils of Chamba districts are the major tribal areas of the state. They are located near the borders of Tibet and Indian States of Jammu and Kashmir.

Other backward areas include Shillai in Sirmaur district, and deep cut-off valleys in the Kullu and upper stretches of Kangradistricts. Due to poor accessibility, life in these areas had grown in isolation.

Kalka-Shimla Railway

History and development

Kinnaur was opened up in the early 1960s with the completion of the Hindustan-Tibet National highway. Lahaul was opened up in the late 1960s with the construction of roads over Rohtang pass. Lahaul is only in contact due to high passes like Rohtang (3,967 m, 13,050 ft), Kunzum (4,600 m, 14,913 ft) and Baralarcha (4,300 m, 14,000 ft). Spiti is a cold desert and is a very underdeveloped area.

The building up of an efficient transport system was the top most priority in the first *Five year plan*. The state has three airports at *Bhuntar* in Kullu district,*Jubbarhatti*near Shimla and *Gaggal* in Kangra. It was only by January 1991 that Himachal was linked up with the broad gauge system by extending the *Delhi-Nangal* rail line. Although railways and airways in Himachal serve very limited transport needs of the people, the road network of the state makes it unique.

Geography

The geography of Himachal presents considerable challenge to the development of transport infrastructure. Nevertheless, the state has made significant progress in road connectivity in the last few decades. Himachal at present has the highest road density among all the hill states of India. Although Himachal also has three airports and two narrow gauge rail tracks, roads remain the main mode of transport in Himachal.

Roads

Roads are the major mode of transport in the hilly terrains. The state has road network of 28,208 kilometres (17,528 mi), including eight National Highways (NH) that constitute 1,234 kilometres (767 mi) and 19 State Highways with a total length of 1,625 kilometres (1,010 mi). Hamirpur district has the highest road density in the country. Some roads get closed during winter and monsoon seasons due to snow and landslides. The state-owned Himachal Road Transport Corporation with a fleet of over 3,100, operates bus services connecting important cities and towns with the villages within the state and also on various interstate routes. In addition, around 3,000 private buses run by various operators also ply in the state.

Eight national highways (NH) pass through the state with a total length of 1235 km. NH 1A touches Shahpur. NH 20 passes through Pathankot, Chakki, Nurpur, Joginder Nagar, Palampur and Mandi. NH 21 connects Chandigarh with Manali through Mandi. NH 22 connects Ambala with Kaurik through Kalka, Simla and Wangtoo. NH 70 passes through Mubarakpur, Amb, Nadaun and Hamirpur. NH 21A begins at Pinjore in Haryana, passes through Nalagarh and reaches Swarghat, where it connects with NH 21. NH 88 connects Simla with Kangra through Hamirpur and Nadaun. NH 72 begins at Ambala and passes through Amb and Paunta Sahib in Himachal Pradesh before terminating at Haridwar in Uttarakhand. The state boasts some of the longest road tunnels in the country namely the 3 km long Aut tunnel in Mandi on NH-21 and the under construction 8.8 km Rohtang tunnel which will create an all year round link between Manali and Lahaul Valley which otherwise remains isolated during its 8 month long winter period.

In addition to the National Highways, the state also has a large mesh of highways and village roads.

Most tourist spots in Himachal Pradesh such as Shimla, Manali, Dharamsala etc. are well connected by roads. Some of the roads in Himachal are seasonal and get closed during winters and monsoons due to heavy snowfall, landslides and washouts.

The Manali-Leh road, for example, remains closed for most part of the winters. The World Bank has approved a loan of $220 million in 2007 to improve priority segments of the state road network.

The government-owned Himachal Road Transport Corporation runs an excellent network of buses interstate and across the state and provides all-weather access to the remotest of the corners of the state.

Himachal Pradesh being a major tourist destination, there is no dearth of private buses and taxis. In spite of state being hilly, Hamirpur District has got highest road density in the country.

Railway

Himachal is known for its narrow-gauge railways. One is the Kalka-Shimla Railway, a UNESCO World Heritage Site, and another is the Pathankot-Jogindernagar line.

The total length of these two tracks is 259 kilometres (161 mi). The Kalka-Shimla Railway passes through many tunnels, while the Pathankot–Jogindernagar meanders through a maze of hills and valleys.

The state also has broad-gauge railway track, which connects Amb and Una (district headquarters of Una district) to Delhi. A survey is being conducted to extend this railway line to Hamirpur. The total route length of the operational railway network in the state is 296.26 kilometres (184.09 mi).Other proposed railways in the state are Dharamsala-Palampur, Baddi-Chandigarh and Bilaspur-Manali-Leh.

Himachal has two narrow-gauge rail tracks. The Kalka-Shimla Railway track has a length of 96 kilometers. It passes through 102 tunnels and crosses 864 bridges. The track has been in existence for over a century now.

Panoramic Kalka-Shimla Railway known to be an engineering marvel of British India. The level of difficulty in laying of tracks could be judged by a journey in the route. The other narrow gauge rail route in the state is the Kangra Valley Railway.

Bilaspur–Mandi–Leh line is a proposed railway project in Himachal Pradesh which will be the longest railway track in the state and is expected to become the highest railway track in the world.

The Kangra Valley Railway covers a distance of 164 km (101.9 mi) from Pathankot, Punjab to Jogindernagar in Himachal Pradesh< between This line is proposed to be converted to broad gauge and further linked to Bilaspur-Mandi line at Mandi.

Both these tracks are commercially unviable but are operated because of their heritage value.

A broad gauge line exists which connects Nangal Dam in Punjab to Una in Himachal Pradesh. Currently this line is being extended till Talwara (Punjab) with track operational till Churu takarla . Una is connected to New Delhi by Jan Shatabdi express and Himachal Express .

Air

The three airports in Himachal Pradesh are: Shimla Airport near Shimla, Gaggal Airport near Kangra and Bhuntar Airport near Kullu. All these airports have runways shorter than 5000 ft and therefore only allow the operation of smaller aircraft such as the Bombardier Dash 8, 70 seater ATR & 42 seater ATR.

Himachal has three domestic airports in Kangra, Kullu and Shimla districts. The air routes connect the state with Delhi and Chandigarh.

- Bhuntar Airport is in Kullu district, around 10 kilometres (6 mi) from district headquarters.
- Gaggal Airport is in Kangra district, around 15 kilometres (9 mi) from district headquarters at Dharamshala, which is around 10 kilometres from Kangra
- Shimla Airport is around 21 kilometres (13 mi) west of the city.

ANIMAL HUSBANDRY

Animal husbandry plays a very major role in the development of agricultural sector of Himachal. Indigenous breeds of cows, buffaloes and sheeps are of very poor quality.

Numerous schemes for *cattle development*, *cattle health* and *disease resistance* in wood production, poultry development, feed and fodder development, dairy improvement, milk supply schemes and veterinary education has been undertaken in order to improve the livestock in the state. There are many veterinary hospitals, dispensaries and outlaying dispensaries in the state to provide veterinary aids and to take measures against various contagious diseases. A number of mobile dispensaries are also in operation.

Recently, Angora rabbits imported from West Germany were introduced in the state. Now 7 units for their propagation have been set up in Kangra.

Milk production has also increased. *Milk chilling plants* with a capacity of about 55,000 liters have been set up at about 24 places and departmental milk supply schemes are operational in 6 towns.

HOSPITALS

From the last 40 years the state has witnessed a lot of improvement in public health facilities. In 1989, there were around 899 public health institutions, including state hospital, twelve district hospitals, 189 primary health centres, besides allopathic and Ayurvedic dispensaries and specialized medical institutions. In order to meet the shortage of doctors, a medical college was established in 1967, which is having post-graduate teaching facilities in some branches.

Death rate has now come down by 70% due to numerous public health measures. The incidence of venereal disease, which was roughly about 17% in 1951, has now came down to 2% in 1989. Diseases like malaria and small pox has been eradicated. The *Tuberculosis control programme* has been a great success. People have taken a keen interest in the family planning programme. One of its interesting feature is that women have outnumbered men in its acceptance.

7

Tourism

TOURISM IN HIMACHAL PRADESH

Tourism in Himachal Pradesh relates to tourism in the Indian state of Himachal Pradesh. Himachal Pradesh is famous for its Himalayan landscapes and popular hill-stations. Many outdoor activities such as rock climbing, mountain biking, paragliding, ice-skating, and heli-skiing are popular tourist attractions in Himachal Pradesh.

Shimla, the state capital, is very popular among tourists. The Kalka-Shimla Railway is a mountain railway which is a UNESCO World Heritage Site. Shimla is also a famous skiing attraction in India. Other popular hill stations include Manali and Kasauli.

Dharamshala, home of the Dalai Lama, is known for its Tibetan monasteries and Buddhist temples. Many trekking expeditions also begin here.

The Ridge is a large road in Shimla which is the centre of most cultural activities of Shimla.

Major attractions

- Shimla
- Manali
- Tattapani

- Spiti valley
- Kasol
- Tosh
- McLeodganj
- Dharamshala
- Kheerganga trek, Parvati Valley
- Paragliding sight (Bir Billing)
- Chamba
- Triund.

Tourism

Kalpa in June 2015

Tourism in Himachal Pradesh is a major contributor to the state's economy and growth. The mountainous state with its Himalayanlandscapes attracts tourists from all over the world. Hill stations like Shimla, Manali, Dharamshala, Dalhousie, Chamba, Khajjiar, Kullu and Kasauli are popular destinations for both domestic and foreign tourists. The state also has many important Hindu pilgrimage sites with prominent temples like Naina Devi Temple, Bajreshwari Devi Temple, Jwala Ji Temple, Chintpurni, Chamunda Devi Temple, Baijnath Temple, Bhimakali Temple, Bijli Mahadev and Jakhoo Temple. Manimahesh Lake situated in the Bharmour region of Chamba district is the venue of an annual Hindu pilgrimage trek held in the month of August which attracts lakhs of devotees. The state is also referred to as *"Dev Bhoomi"* (literally meaning *Abode of Gods*) due to its mention as such in ancient Hindu texts and occurrence of a large number of historical temples in the state.

Triund is a campsite for travellers and trekkers on the way to Indrahar Pass, Dhauladhar Mountain Range.

It is also called the Land of the Gods on account of the Hindu belief that deities like Lord Shiva considered the Himalayas their abode, and much of the state is located among the Himalayan mountains. Although modern pop-literature writers online have often also referred to Uttarakhand as the land of the gods because it also contains Himalayan mountains, officially it is Himachal Pradesh that has been considered the land of the gods since before the state of Uttarakhand existed (the UK as it is abbreviated on license plates for automobiles in the state, and the state was founded in the year 2000). A tourism department board on the road when entering Himachal Pradesh from the state of Punjab states "Welcome to the Land of the Gods."

The state is also known for its adventure tourism activities like ice skating in Shimla, paragliding in Bir Billing and Solang valley, rafting in Kullu, skiing in Manali, boating in Bilaspur and trekking, horse riding and fishing in different parts in the state. Shimla, the state's capital, is home to Asia's only natural ice skating rink. Spiti Valley in Lahaul & Spiti District situated at an altitude of over 3000 metres with its picturesque landscapes is an important destination for adventure seekers. The region also has some of the oldest Buddhist Monasteries in Asia.

Himachal hosted the first Paragliding World Cup in India from 24 October to 31 October in 2015. Venue for paragliding world cup was Bir Billing, which is 70 km from the tourist town Macleod Ganj, located in the heart of Himachal in Kangra District. Bir Billing is the centre for aero sports in Himachal and considered as best for paragliding. Buddhist monasteries, trekking to tribal villages, mountain biking are other activities to do here.

GREAT HIMALAYAN NATIONAL PARK

Great Himalayan National Park (GHNP) is the newest addition to India's national parks, located in Kullu region in the state of Himachal Pradesh. The park was built in the year 1984. The park, is spread over an area of 1,171 sq. km that lies between an altitude of 1500 to 6000m. The Great Himalayan National Park is a habitat to more than 375 fauna species that comprises of nearly around 31 mammals, 181 birds, 3 reptiles, 9 amphibians, 11 annelids, 17 mollusks and 127 insects. They are protected under strict guidelines of Wildlife Protection Act of 1972, hence any sort of hunting is not permitted. It also supports the variety of plant life, scattered over the park.

About the Park: In 1984, the Himachal Wildlife Project (HWP) surveyed the upper Beas region to help establish the boundaries of the park. An area comprising the watersheds of Jiwa, Sainj, and Tirthan rivers became the Great Himalayan

National Park in 1984. Starting from an altitude of 1,700 metres above mean sea level, the highest peak within the Park approaches almost 5,800 metres.

The area of the National Park at the moment is 754.4 km^2 and it is naturally protected on the northern, eastern and southern boundaries by permanent snow or steep ridges. To facilitate conservation a 5 km wide buffer area, extending from the western periphery of the Park, has been classified as the Ecodevelopment Project Area (EPA) or Ecozone.

The EPA has an area of 326.6 km^2 (including 61 km^2 of Tirthan wildlife sanctuary) with about 120 small villages, comprising 1600 households with a population of about 16,000. Since, the Indian Wildlife Protection Act 1972 does not permit any habitation in the National Park, an area of 90 km^2 in Sainj valley encompassing the two villages of Shakti and Marore has been classified as Sainj Wildlife Sanctuary (WLS). These two villages although technically "outside" the National Park, are physically located between two parts of GHNP. Thus the total area under the National Park administration is 1,171 km^2.

Lush coniferous forests, emerald meadows strewn with exotic flora, soaring snowy peaks and pristine glaciers make for an ideal Himalayan retreat. The secluded Sainj and Tirthan valleys are home to a plethora of fauna-wild mountain goats like the bharal, goral and serow, the brown bear and predators like the leopard and the elusive snow leopard. Different varieties of pheasants-monal, khalij cheer, tragopan and other exotic Himalayan birds can be found in the region. The Himalayas have been a source of awe and inspiration for millennia to countless individuals. They are the largest, tallest and geologically youngest mountains on our planet. In India, they are the Dehvbumi—the home of the gods. The Himalaya are also one of the most fragile mountain regions of the world and hold an enormous repository of biological diversity which is increasingly under pressure from human activities.

The unique ecological aspects of the Western Himalaya led to the creation of the Great Himalayan National Park (GHNP) in the Kullu district of India's mountain state of Himachal Pradesh. These features include biodiversity, sparse human populations, inaccessibility, little tourism, and a local economy based on traditional livelihoods.

GHNP is a major source of water for the rural and urban centers of the region with four major rivers of the area originating from the glaciers in the Park. It is also a source of sustenance and livelihood for the local community living close to GHNP. In addition to lumber, the forest environment provides local people with Non-Timber Forest Produce (NTFP) such as honey, fruit nuts, bark of birch and yew, flowers and fuel wood. Globally, as well as locally, the Great Himalayan National Park has a very high public profile.

The international community regards at it as a pilot site where the community based Biodiversity Conservation approach is being tested. The local people in the Ecozone (or Buffer Zone adjacent to the park) of GHNP recognize the fact that they have overexploited the medicinal herbs and NTFPs, and their sheep and goats have overgrazed the pastures.

Park Biogeography: The GHNP is at the junction of world's two major faunal regions: the oriental to the south and palaearctic to the north. The temperate forest flora-fauna of GHNP represents the western most extension of the Sino-Japanese Region. The high altitude ecosystem of the Northwest Himalaya has common plant elements with the adjacent Western and Central Asiatic region.

As a result of its 4,100 m elevation range the Park has a diversity of zones with their representative flora and fauna, such as alpine, glacial, temperate, and sub tropical forests. These biogeographic elements are result of geological evolution of Himalaya which continues today from the action of plate tectonics and continental drift. Over 100 million years ago, the Indian sub-continent broke off from the large, southern landmass, Gondwanaland and moved north.

It eventually slammed into the northern land mass, Laurasia, and formed the gigantic folded mountains of the Himalaya. Due to this union of Gondwanaland and Asiatic landmasses, exchange of flora and fauna was possible and this ultimately led to the unique biogeographical features in the region.

Timeline of Creation: It took twenty years from inception to inauguration for GHNP to be realized as part of the Indian National Park system.

The following is a brief timeline:

1980: Preliminary Park survey of the watersheds of Tirthan, Sainj, and Jiwanal in Banjar area of Kullu district 1983: Continued Park survey, the Banjar area of Kullu district.

1984: Notification by state of Himachal Pradesh of the intention to create the Great Himalayan National Park with buffer zone.

1987: First Management Plan of the Great Himalayan National Park.

1988: Settlement Proceedings and settling of rights of local communities

1992: The Himachal Wildlife Project re-assesses wildlife abundance, livestock grazing, and herb collection and reviewed the existing management plan.

1994: The Government of HP revised the Notification of intention to include the Sainj Wildlife Sanctuary and the upper Parvati watershed.

1994-1999: Conservation of Biodiversity Project (CoB), the Wildlife Institute of India, Dehradun conducts research to assist in the management of the Park.

1999: Declaration of Award upon Completion of Settlement Proceedings. Monetary compensation for individuals who had rights of forest produce in the park area, including a package for providing alternative income generation activities to everybody living in the Ecodevelopment Project Area or Ecozone.

Final Notification of the Great Himalayan National Park. The GHNP becomes the latest and newest National Park of India.

The Conservation of Biodiversity (CoB) Project completed on 31 December 1999.

Park Biodiversity: The Great Himalayan National Park is home to more than 375 faunal species. So far species of 31 mammals, 181 birds, 3 reptiles, 9 amphibians, 11 annelids, 17 mollusks and 127 insects belonging to six orders have been identified and documented. Most of the Himalayan fauna has been given protection under the high priority protection category of Schedule I of the Indian Wildlife (Protection) Act, 1972. The state government of Himachal Pradesh has banned hunting in the state for more than ten years: The ban continues. A trek of 35 to 45 km in any of the Park's valleys brings one into the high altitude habitat (3,500 m and above) of animals such as blue sheep, snow leopard, Himalayan brown bear, Himalayan tahr, and musk deer.

Best sightings can be made in autumn (September-November) as animals start their seasonal migration to lower altitudes. The GHNP also supports a great diversity of plant life thanks to its wide altitude range and relatively undisturbed habitats. From the lofty pines and spruces and the great, spreading horse chestnuts of the lower valleys, to the dense cushions and prostrate branches of the alpine herbs and junipers, the Park presents an endless variety of vegetation.

Although some areas have been modified by grazing, this is one of the few areas of the Western Himalayas where the forests and alpine meadows can be seen in something approaching their original state. The subalpine zone is richest in species, followed by the alpine and upper temperate zones.

Sahara: The Society for Scientific Advancement of Hills & Rural Areas (SAHARA) is a NGO (Non-Governmental Organization) created to address the economic needs of the poor people living in the rural areas adjacent to the Great Himalayan National Park (GHNP). This is an important function since the Park has impacted the lives of these people and they in turn have the potential to impact the Park. The administration of the Indian Park service and that of GHNP in particular have been very supportive of and work closely with SAHARA.

Kalatop Khajjiar Sanctuary: The sanctuary area is well laid out for trekking trails both at Kalatop and Khajjiar. There is a dense Deodar and Fir forest (Dalhousie town) cover. Pheasants, Serow and Black bear are some of the common animals found here. The sanctuary lies in the path of the Ravi River, and is surrounded by coniferous and Oak forests.

- Area-2026.89 hectares (20.27 sq. km).
- Location-District Chamba
- Latitudinal range-32°02′ to 32°04′ N
- Longitudinal range-76°01′ to 76°06′E
- Nearest Town-Dalhousie (06 km)
- Nearest rail gauge-Pathankot (86 km).
- Altitude-1185 to 2768 m
- Temperature-10°C to 35°C
- Mean annual rainfall-672.3 mm.
- Forest cover-1962.84 hectare

BUILDINGS AND STRUCTURES

Hadimba Temple

Legend: According to legends Pandavas, the heroes of the Indian epic 'Mahabharata' stayed in Himachal during their exile. In Manali they were attacked by a powerful 'Rakshsa' (demon) Hadimb, in the ensuing fight Bheem, the strongest of the heroes of this epic, killed the demon. Hadimba was the sister of this demon, she married Bheem and gave birth to Ghatotkach who proved to be a great warrior in the war against Kaurvas.

When Bhim returned to from exile Hadimba did not return with him, but stayed on and did Tapasya (a combination of meditation, prayer and penance) and over a period of time attained the status of Goddess.

Hidimba Devi Temple

Hidimba Devi Temple is at Manali, a hill station in Himachal Pradesh state of north India. This is an ancient cave temple dedicated to Hidimba Devi, a character in the Hindu epic Mahabharata.

The temple is surrounded by a cedar forest at the foot of the Himalaya mountains. The sanctuary is built over a huge rock jutting out of the ground, which was worshipped as an image of the deity. The structure was built in the year 1553.

Design: The Hidimba Devi Temple has intricately carved wooden doors and a wooden shikhara or tower placed above the sanctuary. The wooden temple design is unusual. The tower is 24 metres tall, composed of three square roofs covered in timber tiles and topped by a brass cone-shaped fourth roof. The inside of the temple is occupied by the enormous rock leaving little usable space except for the ground floor. The temple base is whitewashed mud-covered stonework. The main entrance is elaborately carved of wood believed to be over 400 years old. The theme of the carvings is the earth goddess Durgha. However, only a 7.5 cm (3 inch) tall brass image represents the goddess herself. No idol is enshrined.

A rope hangs down that is said to have been used to tie sinners by the hand and swung them against the rock until they were bloody in the presence of the goddess.

Kangra Fort

The Kangra Fort is located 20 kilometers from the town of Dharamsala on the outskirts of the town of Kangra. Situated at a 20 Kilometers distance from Dharamsala on the outskirts of the town of Kangra, India, the fort is thought to date back to 1009 AD.

History: While the fort is thought to date back to 1009 AD, legend has it that it was built by an ally of Kauravas. The fort was heavily damaged in an earthquake in the year 1905. History of the fort is synonmous with that of Kangra town.

Location: The fort is at the beginning of Kangra town. The fort stands on a steep rock in Purana Kangra (translates to Old Kangra) dominating the surrounding valley, built strategically at the "sangam" confluence (places where two rivers meet) of Banganga and Majhi rivers. It is said that Kangra belongs to one who owns the fort. Also near to old kangra is famous jayanti mata temple on a hill top.

Lakkar Bazaar

Lakkar Bazaar is a marketplace adjoining the Ridge in Shimla, India. Shops offer wooden articles targeted mainly towards tourists. There is also a roller skating rink in Lakkar Bazaar. The state hospital known as Indira Gandhi Medical College and hospital is also adjoining to Lakkar Bazaar. Lakkar Bazaar also consists of many hotels such as Hotel White, Diplomat Hotel. One must pass through Lakkar Bazaar while on way to Chapslee Estate, Longwood and Shankli, uptown residential localities of Shimla.

CITIES AND TOWNS

Arki

Arki is a town and a Nagar panchayat in Solan district in the state of Himachal Pradesh, India. The town is notable for its fort built in late 18th century when Arki was the capital of the erstwhile hill state of Baghal.

History: Arki was the capital of the princely hill state of Baghal, which was founded by Rana Ajai Dev, a Panwar Rajput. The state was founded around 1643 and Arki was declared as its capital by Rana Sabha Chand in 1650.

The Arki Fort was built between 1695-1700 by Rana Prithvi Singh, a descendent of Sabha Chand. The Fort was captured by the Gurkhas in 1806. Rana Jagat Singh, the ruler of Baghal had to take refuge in Nalagarh. During this period from 1806-

1815, the Gurkha General Amar Singh Thapa used Arki as his stronghold to make further advances into Himachal Pradesh as far as Kangra.

The Gurkhas were however driven out by Rana Prithvi Singh assisted by Sir David Ochterlony and the British forces during the Gurkha War in 1815-1816. Thereafter Rana Prithvi Singh regained control of Arki. Rana Kishan Singh, who ruled the state from 1840-1867, developed the town of Arki in a planned manner. The Rana was a far sighted ruler and built horse and mule tracks to connect Arki with Shimla and Bilaspur. Many artisans, scholars and businessman from other parts of India settled in Arki during his reign as he provided them with tax free land free of cost.

The Rana was a patron of arts and had muralled interiors installed in the Arki fort in 1850. The murals are a prime attraction among tourists today.

During the Indian Rebellion of 1857, Rana Kishan Singh assisted the British forces for which he was presented the title of *Raja*. Another revolt was suppressed in 1905 with the help of Superintendent of Shimla Hill States.

Geography: Arki is located at 31.15° N 76.97° E. It has an average elevation of 1045 metres (3428 feet).

Arki is located in the Siwalik range of Himalaya mountains. Due to its high altitude, Arki enjoys a pleasant weather in the summers with the temperatures hovering between 26°C-32°C. The winters are chilly and the temperature ranges between 4°C-8°C. The rainfall is moderate and occurs mainly during July and August.

Arki is known for its various caves and cave temples among which *Lutru Mahadev* is very famous.

Sair Fair: The *Sair Fair* is an annual event generally held in Arki around July. The fair is famous for buffalo fights. Local people train their buffalos for the event. The chief guest for the fair in 2005 was Raja Virbhadra Singh, the chief minister of Himachal Pradesh. The fair is attended by thousands of people every year.

Demographics: As of 2001 India census GR India, Arki had a population of 2877. Males constitute 53% of the population and females 47%. Arki has an average literacy rate of 78%, higher than the national average of 59.5%; with 55% of the males and 45% of females literate. 13% of the population is under 6 years of age.

Bilaspur

Bilaspur is a city and a municipal council in Bilaspur District in the state of Himachal Pradesh, India.

Geography: Bilaspur is located at 31.33° N 76.75° E. It has an average elevation of 478 metres (1568 feet). It lies near the reservoir of Govind Sagar on the Sutlej River.

Demographics: As of 2001 India census[GRIndia], Bilaspur had a population of 13,058. Males constitute 53% of the population and females 47%. Bilaspur has an average literacy rate of 83%, higher than the national average of 59.5%; with male literacy of 85% and female literacy of 81%. 10% of the population is under 6 years of age.

History: Bilaspur was the capital of a state founded in the 7th century, and known as Kahlur after its earlier capital, or as Bilaspur after its later capital. The ruling dynasty were Chandela Rajputs, who claimed descent from the rulers of Chanderi in present-day Madhya Pradesh. The town of Bilaspur was founded in 1663.

The state later became a princely state of British India, and was under the authority of the British province of Punjab. In 1932 state was made part of the newly-created Punjab States Agency, and in 1936 the Punjab Hill States Agency was separated from the Punjab States Agency. India became independent in 1947, and on October 12 1948 the ruler acceded to the Government of India. Bilaspur became a separate state of India under a chief commissioner, and on July 1 1954 Bilaspur state was made a district of Himachal Pradesh state by an act of the Indian Parliament.

The historic town was submerged in 1954 when the Sutlej River was dammed to create the Govind Sagar, and a new town was built upslope of the old.

Attractions

- Gobind Sagar
- Institute of Mountaineering and Allied Sport's
- Banda Ridge Top
- Vyas Goofa
- Kot Kahlur

Chamba

Chamba is a town and a municipal council in Chamba district in the state of Himachal Pradesh, India. Chamba town is situated on the banks of the river Ravi which is a tributary of the Trans-Himalayan river Indus. The hub of all activity in Chamba town is the Chaugan, a fine grassy sward, about half a mile long and eighty yards wide, and here is held the Minjar fair, every year, in the month of August. From Chamba one can approach Bharmour famous for it's temples and Manimahesh Kailash, a Hindu pilgrimage spot.

History: Chamba was the ancient Pahari capital and it was established in AD 920 by Raja Sahil Verma who named the settlement after his daughter Champavati.

Geography: Chamba is located at 32.57° N 76.13° E. It has an average elevation of 996 metres (3267 feet).

Demographics: As of 2001 India census[GRIndia], Chamba had a population of 20,312. Males constitute 52% of the population and females 48%. Chamba has an average literacy rate of 81%, higher than the national average of 59.5%; with male literacy of 85% and female literacy of 77%. 10% of the population is under 6 years of age.

Dalhousie Cantonment

Dalhousie is a cantonment town in Chamba district in the state of Himachal Pradesh, India.

Geography: Dalhousie is located at 32.53° N 75.98° E. It has an average elevation of 1954 metres (6410 feet).

Demographics: As of 2001 India census[GRIndia], Dalhousie had a population of 1962. Males constitute 56% of the population and females 44%. Dalhousie has an average literacy rate of 76%, higher than the national average of 59.5%: male literacy is 79% and, female literacy is 72%. In Dalhousie, 14% of the population is under 6 years of age.

Dharamsala

Geography: Dharamsala is located at 32.22° N 76.32° E. It has an average elevation of 1457 metres (4780 feet).

Dharamsala is located in the Kangra valley, in the Dhauladhar mountains. It became the capital of the Kangra District in 1852.

History: Dharamsala has been connected with Hinduism and Buddhism for a long time, with many monasteries having been established there in the past, built by Tibetan immigrants in the 8th century, however, these monasteries are believed to have declined, with traditional Hindu building styles experiencing a revival.

The local Gaddi people are now almost all Hindu, and for the most part worship many gods and goddesses, principally Durga and Shiva.

In 1848, the area was annexed by the British, and a year later, a military garrison was established in the town. Dharamsala eventually became the administrative capital of Kangra District in 1852.

It became a popular hill station for the British working in or near Delhi, offering a cool respite during the hot summer months.

However, the town was virtually destroyed in a massive earthquake in 1905, which killed an estimated 20,000 people. Not only the town was devastated, but the nearby town Kangra was also ruined. After this, the British moved their summer headquarters to Shimla (also written Shimla) which, though not far away, is off the main fault line and, therefore, less likely to experience a serious earthquake. Dharamsala still experiences frequent minor earthquakes.

When the Dalai Lama left Tibet, Indian Prime Minister Jawaharlal Nehru offered to permit him and his followers to establish a "government-in-exile" in Dharamsala in 1960. Since then, many Tibetan exiles have settled in the town, numbering several thousand.

Most of these exiles live in Upper Dharamsala, or McLeod Ganj, where they established monasteries, temples and schools. The town is sometimes known as "Little Lhasa", after the Tibetan capital city, and has become an important tourist destination with many hotels and restaurants, creating a resurgence in tourism and commerce.

Since 2002, Dharamsala has hosted a Miss Tibet beauty contest.

Demographics: As of the 2001 India census[GRIndia], Dharmsala had a population of 19,034. Males constitute 55% of the population and females 45%. Dharmsala has an average literacy rate of 77%, higher than the national average of 59.5%: male literacy is 80% and, female literacy is 73%. In Dharamsala, 9% of the population is under 6 years of age.

The natural features surrounding the town include rich forests of pine and deodars.

The town is divided between Upper Dharamsala or McLeod Ganj (which retains a British colonial atmosphere), and Lower Dharamsala (the commercial centre). Upper Dharamsala (elevation about 1,700 m or 5,580 ft.) is about 9 kilometers (5.6 miles) from Lower Dharmsala by road and is some 460 m (1,510 ft.) higher.

McLeod Ganj, or Upper Dharamsala, is the residence of Tenzin Gyatso, the current Dalai Lama. A substantial community of Tibetan exiles resides in the town. There is a small Anglican church, St. John of the Wilderness, featuring stained-glass windows, just a few hundred metres from McLeod Ganj.

The area covered by Dharamsala is almost 29 km^2. During the months of December and January, snowfall and hail is common and the temperature ranges from 0 °C to 14.5 °C. During summers, the temperature ranges from 22 °C to 38 °C.

There is an airport about 20 km away, in Kangra, 5 Kms away. Rice, wheat and tea are grown around Dharamsala.

8

Population and Religion

POPULATION OF HIMACHAL PRADESH 2018

Himachal Pradesh is an excellent state in North India. It is flanked by Jammu and Kashmir, Punjab and by the Tibet Autonomous Region on the east. Hima suggests snow in Sanskrit and the strict significance of the state's name is in the lap of the Himalayas.

It was named by Acharya Diwakar Datt Sharma, he was a standout among the most acclaimed Sanskrit scientists of Himachal Pradesh.

The state is well known for its Himalayan scenes, incline stations and havens. Himachal Pradesh has been situated fifteenth in the list of the most noteworthy per capita salaries of the states and union territories for 2013-14. There are various conduits gushing in the state with hydroelectric activities set up.

Population Of Himachal Pradesh In 2018

The state has an aggregate population of 6,864,602 including 3,481,873 males and 3,382,729 females according to the last results of the Census of India 2011. In the enumeration, the state is set 21st on the population chart.

Talking about population, in order to check out the population of Himachal Pradesh in 2018, we need to have a look at the population of the past 5 years. They are as per the following:

1. 2013 – 6.92 Million
2. 2014 – 7.1 Million
3. 2015 – 7.34 Million
4. 2016 – 7.5 Million
5. 2017 – 7.6288 Million

Predicting the 2018 population of Himachal Pradesh is not easy but we can get the idea after analysing the population from the year 2013 – 17. As we have seen that every year the population increases by approximate 0.14176 Million people. Hence, the population of Himachal Pradesh in 2018 is forecast to be 7.6288 Million + 0.14176 Million = 7.77056 Million. So, the population of Himachal in the year 2018 as per estimated data is 7.77056 Million.

Himachal Pradesh Population 2018 –7.77056 Million. (estimated).

Demography Of Himachal Pradesh

The life expectancy is 62.8 years for 1986–1990. The child death rate stayed at 40 in the year 2010 and the birth rate has declined from 37.3 to 16.9 in 2010. Hindi is both the official tongue and the most generally utilized dialect of Himachal Pradesh. Regardless, most of the people speaks Pahari in consistent discussion, which fuses all Western Pahari languages. There are about 32 dialects in Himachal.

Population Density And Growth Of Himachal Pradesh

The population density of the state is 123 persons per square kilometre. It has enrolled 12.81% growth in terms of population in the midst of the earlier decade while the female sex proportion subtly upgraded from 968 to 974. The state, which was segmented with Gujarat, Punjab and Haryana for low female sex proportion in 0-6 year age gathering, mostly adjusted the course and recorded enhanced sex proportion of 906 in the year of 2011 data records against 896 out of 2001.

Facts About Himachal Pradesh:

1. There are 33 Sanctuaries and 2 National Parks of which The Great Himalayan National Park has been declared as a noteworthy site by the UNESCO.
2. Kasol is notable by the name of Mini Israel possibly because of its most noteworthy tourists being that of Israeli origin. In this manner most of the shops and motels too have written stuff in Hebrew. Furthermore, the garments of clothing and food, especially pita bread and hummus similarly give you the feeling of being in Israel.
3. It holds the title of being the second least corrupted province of India after Kerala.
4. Himachal has some outstanding boarding schools that are moreover the oldest running schools since they were set up in the midst of the British time.
5. The Kalka-Shimla express goes through a gigantic extend of 806 platforms, 103 passages and 18 stations.

DEMOGRAPHICS

Population

Himachal Pradesh has a total population of 6,864,602 including 3,481,873 males and 3,382,729 females as per the final results of the Census of India 2011. This is only 0.57 per cent of India's total population, recording a growth of 12.81 per cent. The scheduled castes and scheduled tribes account for 25.19 per cent and 5.71 per cent of the population respectively. The sex ratio stood at 972 females per 1000 males, recording a marginal increase from 968 in 2001. The child sex ratio increased from 896 in 2001 to 909 in 2011. The total fertility rate (TFR) per woman in 2015 stood at 1.7, one of the lowest in India.

In the census, the state is placed 21st on the population chart, followed by Tripura at 22nd place. Kangra district was top ranked with a population strength of 1,507,223 (21.98%), Mandi district 999,518 (14.58%), Shimla district 813,384 (11.86%), Solan district 576,670 (8.41%), Sirmaur district 530,164 (7.73%), Una district 521,057 (7.60%), Chamba district518,844 (7.57%), Hamirpur district 454,293 (6.63%), Kullu district 437,474 (6.38%), Bilaspur district 382,056 (5.57%), Kinnaur district 84,298 (1.23%) and Lahaul Spiti 31,528 (0.46%).

The life expectancy at birth in Himachal Pradesh increased significantly from 52.6 years in the period from 1970-75 (above the national average of 49.7 years) to 72.0 years for the period 2011-15 (above the national average of 68.3 years). The infant mortality rate stood at 40 in 2010, and the crude birth rate has declined from 37.3 in 1971 to 16.9 in 2010, below the national average of 26.5 in 1998. The crude death rate was 6.9 in 2010. Himachal Pradesh's literacy rate has almost doubled between 1981 and 2011. The state is one of the most literate states of India with a literacy rate of 83.78% as of 2011.

RELIGION

The bulk population of Himachal Pradesh is Hindus, 95.77% of the total population (1981 census).

The Muslims occupy the second position 1.63%. They have some concentration in Chamba, Kangra and Sirmur. The Buddhists constitute a little more than 1% of the population and live in the trans-himalayan areas of Lahaul and Spiti, Kinnaur and Kulu while the Sikhs (1.2%) are found here and there with some concentration in Kangra, Shimla, Mandi and Sirmur districts. The Christian population is 0.1%.

The people are deeply religious and god fearing. The grandeur of the natural features, the Himalayas and the magnitude of physical forces, has led the inhabitants to assign supernatural powers to natural environments. To the children of the mountains, the' Himalayas are the Gods'. Along with the Gods represented in the 'Thakardwara's' and the 'Shivalas', people worship the village deities, the Deotas, the Rishis, the Munis, the Siddhas, the Pandavas, the hill tops, the trees, the joginis or wood fairies, the Kali, the Shakti, the Nagas (snakes) and even a host of devils and deities of the aborigines. They believe that water courses, the sprouting seeds, the ripening corn ear are all in charge of separate spirits. Animals sacrifice is a major religious rite and is performed at weddings, funerals, festivals, harvest time, on the beginning of the thanksgiving.

Lamaistic Buddhism is practiced in the trans-himalayan areas. The great Padma Sambhava who was responsible for the spread of Buddhism in Tibet in the 8th century, lived for sometime at Riwalsar near Mandi. There is a temple in his name. Lamaistic Buddhism assimilates the mysticism of the northern school of Buddhism, the 'Vajra-yana' with the magic and devil worship of the Tantras and the cult of the Shakti, Tara. The priest or the Lama is the friend, philosopher and guide of the Buddhists. He guides them in spiritual matters, foretells events, determines lucky and unlucky days, practices medicine, exorcises evil spirits, performs magic and regulates the destiny of the living and the dead.

The Muslims in the villages follow Saint Pir Lakh Data and also pray and light earthen lamps at the shrines of other saints.

Religion in Himachal Pradesh (2011)

Hinduism (95.17%)

Islam (2.18%)

Sikhism (1.16%)

Buddhism (1.15%)

Christianity (0.18%)

Jainism (0.03%)

Other or none (0.2%)

Hinduism is the major religion in Himachal Pradesh. More than 95% of the total population adheres to the Hindu faith, the distribution of which is evenly spread throughout the state. Himachal Pradesh has the highest proportion of Hindu population among all the states and union territories in India.

Other religions that form a small percentage are Islam, Sikhism and Buddhism. Muslims are mainly concentrated in

Sirmaur, Chamba, Una and Solan districts where they form 2.53-6.27% of the population. Sikhs mostly live in towns and cities and constitute 1.16% of the state population. The Buddhists, who constitute 1.15%, are mainly natives and tribals from Lahaul and Spiti, where they form a majority of 62%, and Kinnaur, where they form 21.5%.

BUDDHISM IN HIMACHAL PRADESH

Buddhism in the Indian state of Himachal Pradesh can be traced back to the spread of Buddhism in the early 8th century. Over the centuries the practice of Buddhism has become deeper rooted in the region, particularly in the Lahaul, Spiti and Kinnaur valleys of Himachal Pradesh. After the 14th Dalai Lama, Tenzin Gyatso, escaped from Tibet with his followers in 1959 and took refuge in India, the focus on Tibetan Buddhism spread further and attracted immense international sympathy and support. The Dalai Lama found Dharamshala in Himachal Pradesh as an ideal place to establish his "capital in exile" at McLeod Ganj in close vicinity to Dharamshala, and is called the Little Lhasa and also as Dhasa (a combination of Dharamshala and Lhasa in Tibet). This situation has given the state a unique status in the global firmament of Buddhist traditions. It is now the cradle of Tibetan Buddhism, with its undeniable link to the past activities initiated in the 8th century (in 747 AD) by Guru Padmasambhava (who went to Tibet from Rewalsar in Himachal Pradesh in North India to spread Buddhism), who was known as the "Guru Rinpoche" and the "Second Buddha".

The influence of Buddhism is strong throughout the Trans-Himalayan region or Western Himalayas, formed by the Indian states of Jammu and Kashmir and Himachal Pradesh and bounded by the Indus River on the extreme west and the Tons-Yamuna River gorge on the east. With the influx of Tibetan refugees into India, in the last over 50 years (since 1959), popularity and practice of Tibetan Buddhism has been notable. Apart from the original practitioners of Tibetan Buddhism in ancient and medieval India, it is now seriously pursued by

Tibetans re-settled at Dharamshala (the nodal centre and the 'capital in exile' of the Dalai Lama were initially re-settled) in Himachal Pradesh, Dehradun (Uttar Pradesh), Kushalnagar (Karnataka), Darjeeling (West Bengal), Arunachal Pradesh, Sikkim and Ladakh.

Overview

After a lull in the spread of Buddhism in the state during the 10th century, the Tibetan King Yeshe Od of Guge took the initiative to revive it. Of the 21 scholars he had sent to revive Buddhism in the Trans Himalayan region, only two had survived, and one of them was the famous scholar-translator Rinchen Zangpo who transfused Buddhist activity in the state of Himachal Pradesh. Known by the epithet "Lohtsawa" or the "Great Translator", Zangpo built 108 monasteries in the trans-Himalayan region to spread Buddhism, which are considered as the main stay of Vajrayana of Tibetan Buddhism (also known as Lamaism). He institutionalised Buddhism in this region. Zangpo had engaged Kashmiri artists who created wall paintings and sculptures in these legendary 108 monasteries; only a few of these have survived in Himachal Pradesh namely, the Lhalung Monastery, Nako Gompa in Spiti and Tabo Monastery in Spiti, the last named monastery is known as the Ajanta of the Himalayas. In Himachal Pradesh, apart from these ancient Buddhist monasteries set up by Zangpo, his contemporaries of other Buddhist sects built many more monasteries. This activity thus further continued in the subsequent centuries under the four main traditions of Nyingma, Kagyu, Gelug, and Sakya, categorised as per teachings into three "vehicles":Hinayana, Mahayana, and Vajrayana. These monasteries are mostly in the Spiti, Lahaul and Kinnaur valleys. Some of the well known monasteries are Gandhola Monastery (Drukpa Kargyu sect) Guru Ghantal Monastery, Kardang Monastery (Drukpa sect), Shashur Monastery, Tayul Monastery and Gemur Monastery in the Lahaul Valley, Dhankar Monastery, Kaza Monastery, Kye Monastery, Tangyud Monastery (Sakya sect), Kungri Monastery (of the Nyingmasect), Kardang Monastery (Drukpa

Kagyu sect) and Kibber Monastery in the Spiti Valley, and the Bir Monasteries (Bir Tibetan monasteries of the Nyingma, Kagyu and Sakya sects) in the Kangra valley.

History

Kalachakra Temple

The very earliest influence of Buddhism in Himachal Pradesh is traced to the Ashokan period in the 3rd century BC. He had established many stupas, and one of them was traced to the state in the Kulu valley, as cited in the chronicles of the Chinesetravellers. Mention is also made of a much earlier propagation during Buddha's time itself by Sthavira Angira and Stavira Kanakavatsa, in the Kailash area and Kashmir respectively. In the 7th century, King Songtsen Gampo of Tibet had deputed Thomi Sambota to visit Buddhist Viharas in India to imbibe more of Indian Buddhist knowledge. It was in 749 AD that Padmasambhava (hailed as the second Buddha) with his compatriot Shantarakshita established the Vajrayana Buddhism in the Western Himalayan region.Rewalsar lake at Rewalsar in Mandi district is where Padmasambhava (literal meaning "lotus born") is said to have meditated for long years. At Rewalsar, there is also a strange legend of his life linked to the local King, his daughter and the lake. It is one of the most ancient links to Tibetan Buddhism in Himachal Pradesh where Buddhists undertake parikrama of the lake on religious pilgrimage.

Archaeological evidence in Himachal Pradesh offers strong evidence of Buddhist influence. Numismatic evidence has established the presence of Buddhism in the Kuluta region (upper Beas region of the Kuluta Kingdom) of the state in the 1st century BC and 2nd century AD. On the Palampur-Malan-Dadh-Dharamshala road,2.5 kilometres (1.6 mi) from Malan rock inscriptions in Brahmi and Kharoshti scripts of 3rd and 2nd century BC have been discovered on a single granite rock known as *Lakhina pathar*, which are supported by the Buddhist monuments at Chahri; inscribed pedestals of Vajravarahi (Buddhist tantric goddess) is dated to 5th or early 6th century. Handa's archaeological explorations have also unearthed a headless stone image of Buddha (now in the Kangra Museum) at sites of Chetru and Kanhiara villages; Chetru in local lingua is interpreted as Chaitya in Sanskrit. Names such as Matth and Trilokinath and dozen maths in Kangra and Mandi districts further point to Buddhist establishments between the 3rd century BC and 6th century AD. Cave type (*guha* type) Buddhist monastery at Gandhala has been inferred from a copper lot (pot), chased with Jataka episode discovered in a monastic cell in Kullusubdivision of the Kangra division which is dated to the 2nd century AD. Trilokinath and Gandhala (also known as

Guru Ghantal), beyond Rohtang la pass are considered classical Buddhist shrines of Indian Buddhism (inferred to predate Padmasmbhava's times by many centuries). Discovery of marble head (7th or 8th century AD) of Avalokiteshvara at the confluence of Chandra and Bhagha Rivers support evidence of monastic activities in these remote regions.

Archaeological evidence also supports the influence of Vajrayana Buddhism influence prior to the 8th century in the region east of Sutlej river. Cult powers of Padmasambhava, before he went to Tibet (before 747 AD), are also deciphered from legends at Nako in Kinnaur, Trilokinath and Gandhala in Lahaul, and Rewalsar in Mandi district. From the mid 8th century (after 747 AD) evidence of Buddhist activities remain obscure till Tibetan Buddhism penetrated the region in the 10th century.

Rinchen Zangpo was urged by Buddhist Guru Shantarakshita from Kashmir, who had already established a monastic order in Tibet, to travel around to spread Buddhism in the trans-Himalayan region. At that time, Zangpo was teaching in Kashmir. He embarked on his campaign to teach Buddhism in the trans-Himalayan region by travelling through Lahaul, Spiti and Kinnaur valleys of the Sutlej River valley, in Himachal Pradesh, then to Ladakh and further on to Tibet, Nepal, Sikkim and Bhutan. He established Buddhist Dharma in all these regions. This period was called the "Second Coming" of Buddhism in the region since earlier efforts made had not progressed much. It is said that Zangpo's persistence of amalgamating Tibetan Buddhism into the Indian creed was the "Second Advancement" or "Second Coming", also called the "Classical Period". Since then, Tibetan Buddhism has also imbibed many of the religious practices and culture of India. Buddhist monastic art and architecture thus went through a sea change.

Another Buddhist Tantric Guru Deepankara Srijnana (Atisha) (982–1054) was held in high esteem during the period of Zangpo. He had a great influence on Zangpo in teaching the finer aspects of Tantric texts in Sanskrit and the translated texts in Tibetan. Under Atisha's influence there was conceptual reformation of primitive Buddhism in Tibet into the Mahayana Buddhism, which laid stress on "celibacy and morality". This resulted in the evolution of a reformed sect known as Kahdampa, which eventually got subsumed under the Gelukpa sect.

This reformation also caused further break-up of Buddhism under several sects and sub sects. The Kings of Guge had a significant role in propagation of the religion, which had strong influence on the architectural planning of Tibetan monasteries. One of the Guge brothers, Chang chub-O, had even got the Tabo Monastery in Spiti refurbished.

But Tibet was fragmented under the influence of its various sects and subsects, which attracted Mongol invasion. Three events in the 13th century had profound effect on Tibetan Buddhism; one was Chengiz Khan's invasion of Tibet in 1206; the second event in the second half of thirteenth century was that of the then Chinese ruler Kublai Khan's (of Yunan, who later became a Buddhist); and the third of Kashmir, which until then had been a stronghold of Buddhism, going under Muslim rule after 1339, putting an end to cultural communication with India. Mongol invasion is also credited with uniting Tibet under the institution of the Dalai Lama.

While the Mongols favoured the Sakya sect, the Ming dynasty (Chinese) favoured Kargyupa and Kahdampa sects; but these actions resulted in inter-sectoral rivalry and even destruction of each other's monasteries. It was during this period that monasteries were also built on hilltops and many were also well fortified. The period between 1300 AD and 1850 AD marked the development of hill-top monasteries and examples of this type in the western Himalayan region are the Ki Monastery in Spiti and the Hemis Monastery in Ladakh.

Thus, from the 14th century onwards, the monasteries had adopted a fort-like design for its buildings from logistic considerations and built them as "religio-military strongholds"; many of them have disappeared due to invasions but some have survived in Ladakh and Spiti valleys in India. Zangpo's "Classical monasteries" in Western Tibet, in Lahaul, Spiti and Kinnaur in Himachal Pradesh, and in Ladakh have survived and are fairly well preserved for posterity. However, instances of greed and neglect have been reported in some monasteries.

Tibetan immigration

The Khadamp sect, which was reorganised as "Gelukpa sect" at the start of the 15th century by Tsongkhapa has dominated Tibet and became the "Spiritual and Temporal Authority of Tibet" with the Dalai Lama invested with full authority of this sect. While the founder Lama of Gelukpa sect was Tsongkhapa, his nephew Gendun Drup was the first Grand Lama and since then the mantle has been passed on to the subsequent Lamas under a Reincarnation theory of succession. The fifth Dalai Lama subsumed all of the other sub-sects under his control, with his headquarters at Lhasa as the supreme head of Buddhism in Tibet. The Dalai Lamas also held some political power in certain areas of Tibet until the 14th Dalai Lama emigrated to India in 1959.

The 14th Dalai Lama established his "Government in exile", in 1960 at Mcleod Ganj in the upper part of the town of Dharamshala. This has since become the nerve centre of Tibetan Buddhism with the Tibetan refugees establishing monasteries of their sects, such as the Gelukpa, Sakyapa, Kargyupa, Nyingmapa, Chonangpa and Dragung-Kargyupa; Non-Buddhist of Bön religion also have established their monastery here. Over 40 monasteries (unofficial records) of these sects have been reported.

In order to educate ethnic Tibetan youths in Dharamshala and the Himalayan border students of India, the Central Institute of Higher Tibetan Studies (CIHTS) was established at Varanasi by Pt. Jawahar Lal Nehru in consultation with the Dalai Lama. The Institute, a Deemed University since 1988, is currently headed by Prof. Ngawang Samten, assisted by faculty members of the Institute. Its primary goal is to achieve excellence in the field of Tibetology, Buddhology and Himalayan Studies.

EARLIEST LAKE AND MONASTERIES

The earliest reverential link according to Padmasmabhava's legend is to the Rewalsar lake at Rewalsar in Mandi district of Himachal Pradesh where Padmasambhava is said to have meditated. There are three monasteries located here namely, the ancient Nyingmapa Monastery on periphery of the Rewalsar lake and two new monasteries (of modern construction) namely, the Drigung Kagyu Monastery (a multistoreyed complex behind the ancient monastery) of the Kagyu order and Tso-Pema Ogyen Heru-kai Nyingmapa Gompa.

Rewalsar

Rewalsar has an ancient divine link for the Buddhists as it is believed that Guru Padmasambhava set out from here on his journey to Tibet to propagate Buddhist dharma. The Rewalsar Lake ('Tso Pema' or 'Pad-ma-can' to Tibetans) has a legend that started the belief that on the islands of floating reeds of the lake the spirit of Padmasambhava's resides. According to folk legend, Padmasmabhava tried to teach Buddhist dharma to the daughter (Mandarava) of the King of Mandi, Arshadhara of Sahor, which was seriously resented by the King. It is also mentioned that Mandarva was enamoured of Padmasambhava of Nalanda. The King, therefore, ordered Padmasambhava to be burnt alive. However, the pyre burned for a full week, with great clouds of black smoke arising from it and a lake appeared there after a week at the spot where he was supposed to have been burnt. Then, Padmasambhava (also known as Vajracharya), unscathed by the fire, is said to have appeared seated on a full-blown lotus from within a lotus in the middle of the lake. One version states that the King, as a repentance for his wrong actions, married his daughter with Padmasambhava. Another version states that Mandarava (stated to be the sister of Shantarakshita) as repentance, left her parents' house, and meditated near a well, which has now become a shrine (worshipped by Tibetan Buddhists as a manifestation of Shakthi). It was from this lake that Padmasambhava travelled to Tibet to spread the Vajrayana

Buddhism. Rawalsar has two monasteries, namely, the Drikung Kagyu Gompa and Tso-Pema Ogyen Heru-kai Nyingmapa Gompa.

To commemorate Padmasmabahava (so named after he emerged from the Padmacan lake or lotus lake), a monastery was built on the western shore of the lake, called the Nyingmapa Monastery (built in Central Tibetan fashion), which has been expanded manifold into a multistoreyed pagoda type structure, with several renovations done till the late 19th century. A large gilded statue of Padmasambahava in the formal attire as the manifestation of Guru Rinpoche is deified here. There are two other new monasteries built around the ancient monastery; these are the Drigung Kagyu Monastery of the Kagyupa order and the other monastery called the Tso-Pema Ogyen Heru-kai Nyingmapa Gompa of the Nyingma sect; though of modern construction these two have retained the aesthetic Tibetan architectural ambience.

In 2004, to commemorate the birthday of Padmasambhava, the Tsechu fair was held here, after a gap of 12 years. The fair was inaugurated by the Dalai Lama and was attended by Urgyen Trinley Dorje Karmapa along with 50,000 other Buddhist pilgrims. The Dalai Lama also performed a parikrama (circumambulation) of the lake.

Rinchen Zangpo's monasteries

Rinchen Zangpo, the famous scholar-translator, established 108 monasteries during his mission undertaken in the 10th century to propagate Buddhist Dharma in the Trans-Himalayan region. A few of them, which have survived in Himachal Pradesh, present exquisite monasteries of artistic and architectural excellence in Lahaul, Spiti and Kinnaur valleys of the Sutlej River valley, such as the Tabo monastery, Lhalung monastery and Nako monastery.

Tabo monastery

Tabo Monastery (or Tabo Chos-Khor Monastery) was founded in 996 AD (and refurbished in 1042 AD) by Rinchen Zangpo; it is considered the oldest monastery in Himachal Pradesh. It located at the southern edge of the Trans Himalayan plateau in the Spiti Valley on the banks of the Spiti River, in the very arid, cold and rocky area at an altitude of 3,050 metres (10,010 ft). The sprawling monastery, spread over an area of 6,300 square metres (68,000 sq ft), has nine temples – the Temple of the Enlightened Gods (gTug-Lha-khang), the Golden Temple (gSer-khang), the Initiation Temple (dKyil-kHor- khang), the Bodhisattva Maitreya Temple (Byams-Pa Chen-po Lha-khang), the Temple of Dromton (Brom-ston Lha khang), the Chamber of Picture Treasures (Z'al-ma), the Large Temple of Dromton (Brom-ston Lha khang), the Mahakala Vajra Bhairava Temple (Gon-khang) and the White Temple (dKar-abyum Lha-Khang) (out of these nine, the first four are considered the oldest temples while the others were later additions) – 23 chortens, monks' residences and an extension that houses the nuns' residence. It was initially an important centre of learning of the Kadampa order, which later developed into the Gelukpa order. It was severely damaged in the 1975 Kinnaur earthquake and has since been re-built with a new *Dukhang* (assembly hall). The Dalai Lama held the Kalachakra ceremonies here in 1983 and 1996. The year 1996 marked 1000 years of Tabo Monastery's existence. A number of caves carved into the cliff face are located above the monastery, which are used by monks for meditation. The monastery is studded with large collection of precious Thangka (scroll paintings), manuscripts, well-preserved statues, frescos and extensive murals that cover almost every wall. The monastery is a national historic treasure of India and preserved by the Archaeological Survey of India.

The few original paintings of Bodhisattvas, from the period of the renovation of Tabo monastery in 1042, seen in the Dukong (assembly hall), are similar in style to those seen at Alchi Monastery in its aesthetic elegance. These have a gentle form with stress on unique detailing of textiles and ornaments. The paintings in the assembly hall are dedicated to Vairochana. Also seen are paintings of two narrative sequences namely, the first narrative is about the visit by Sudhana, a merchant's son, deputed by Bodhisattva Manjushri, on a spiritual mission, while the second narrative depicts the life of the Buddha. The Dalai Lama has expressed his desire to retire to Tabo, since he maintains that the Tabo Monastery is one of the holiest.

It is a World Heritage Site listed by UNESCO. Its sanctity in the Trans Himalayan Buddhism is considered as second only to that of the Tholing Monastery in Tibet.

Lhalung monastery

Lhalung Monastery, Lhalun Monastery or Lalung Monastery (also known as the Sarkhang or Golden Temple), one of the earliest monasteries (considered second to Tabo monastery in importance) founded in Spiti valley, near the Lingti river. It is dated to the late 10th century and credited to Rinchen Zangpo. Village of Lhalung (meaning: 'land of the gods') in the vicinity of the monastery, at an altitude of 3,658 metres (12,001 ft), has 45 homes. A few chortens are located on the way to the monastery. It is said that the Lhalung Devta is head of all the Devtas of the valley and emerges from the Tangmar mountain beyond the village. It was a complex of nine shrines enclosed within a dilapidated wall with the main chapel richly decorated. The monastery is inferred as an ancient centre of learning and debate (local name: *Choshore*) on the basis of old ruins of several temples seen around the five buildings of the monastery, apart from an equally ancient sacred tree. Serkhang, the golden hall of the temple complex has is studded with images (most of them gilded) of deities (51 deities) – mounted on walls or erected on a central altar.

Nako monastery

The Nako monastery is located (3,660 metres (12,010 ft)) near the India-China border in the trans-Himalayan region in Nako village in Kinnaur district at its western edge. The monastery complex in the village has four temples in an enclosure built with mud walls. It is also dated to the second coming of Buddhism to the region and is credited to Rinchen Zangpo. The area is known for the Nako Lake, which forms part of the border of the village.

Though the monastery complex looks simple from outside, in the interiors of the complex, the wall paintings in the monastery are delicately executed. Influence of the Ajanta style of painting, is distinct "in the tonal variation of body hues to produce an effect of light and shade". The elegant divine figures have placid expressions, a reflection of the finest classical art of India.

The four temples are well preserved; the main temple and the upper temple considered the oldest of the four structures have the original clay sculptures, murals and ceiling panels – larger temple of these two is known as the 'Translator's Temple'; the third structure is a small white temple, partly dilapidated, has a wooden door frame depicting scenes of the Life of the Buddha carved on the lintel; and the fourth structure is of the same size as the Upper Temple and is also situated next to it, which is known as "rGya-dpag-pa'i lHa-khang" meaning temple of wide proportions.

An impression of a foot found near the Nako Lake is ascribed to Guru Padmasambhava. In a nearby village called Tashigang, several caves are found where it is said Guru Padmasambhava meditated and gave discourse to his disciples. An image is stated to grow hair.

Fourteenth century and later monasteries

The trend of building fortified Buddhist monasteries was started from the 14th century onwards. However, very few have survived. Of these, Tangyud monastery, Dhankar monastery and Key monastery in Spiti valley are some of the well known ones.

Tangyud Monastery

The Tangyud Monastery in the Spiti valley was built in the early 14th century when the Sakyapas rose to power under Mongol patronage. It is built like a fortified castle on the edge of a deep canyon, with massive slanted mud walls and battlements with vertical red ochre and white vertical stripes which make them look much taller than they really are. It is at an altitude of 4,587 metres (15,049 ft), on the edge of a deep canyon and overlooking the town of Kaza, 4 kilometres (2.5 mi) from the town. It is one of only two monasteries belonging to the Sakya sect left in Spiti – the other, at Kaza itself, is small and relatively insignificant. It is thought, however, that there was an earlier Kadampa establishment here founded by Rinchen Zangpo (958–1055 AD) and named *Rador-lha*.

Castle type Tangyud Monastery, Spiti valley.

Inside Assembly Hall, Tangyud Monastery, Spiti

The name, Tangyud, may refer to the Sakya revision of the *Tang-rGyud*, or the 87 volumes of Tantra treatises which form part of the Tengyur; this was done around 1310 AD by a team of scholars under the Sakya lama, Ch'os-Kyi-O'd-zer. The unplanned arrangement of the monastery is attributed to several modifications carried out after it was ransacked by invasions of Central Tibet by Mongols, in 1655 AD. The monastery is also famous for the expertise of the Sakyapa tantric cult that even dacoits are scared to rob this monastery.

Dhankar Monastery

Dhankar Monastery – a Fort monastery at 3,894 metres (12,776 ft) altitude.

Dhankar Monastery also spelt Drangkhar or Dhangkar Gompa; *Brang-mkhar* or *Grang-mkhar*, situated in the Spiti Valley between the towns of Kaza and Tabo at an elevation of 3,894 metres (12,776 ft) is a fort monastery similar to the Key Monastery and Tangyud Monastery in Spiti built in the Central Tibetan pattern. Dhankar was the traditional capital of the

Spiti Valley Kingdom during the 17th century. The complex is built on a 300 metres (980 ft) high spur overlooking the confluence of the Spiti River and Pin River – one of the world's most spectacular settings for a gompa. *Dhang* or *dang* means cliff, and *kar* or *khar* means fort.

Prayer flags in Dhankar Monastery

Hence, Dhangkar means *fort on a cliff*. It belongs to the Gelukpa order but claims to its earlier founding in the 12th century has put forth by the local monks. Below this Gompa is the small village of Shichilling where the new Dhankar Monastery has been built. It is home to about 150 monks belonging to the Gelukpa sect of Tibetan Buddhism. Dhankar is approachable by a road, good for small vehicles only, that branches off for Dhankar from the main Kaza-Samdu road at a point around 24 kilometres (15 mi) from Kaza.

In 2006, World Monuments Fund selected Dhankar gompa as one of the 100 most endangered sites in the world. A non-profit group, Dhangkar Initiative, is attempting to organize its conservation.

Key Monastery

The earliest history of Key Monastery is traced to Dromtön (Brom-ston, 1008–1064 CE), a pupil of the famous teacher, Atisha, in the 11th century.

This however, refers to destroyed Kadampa monastery at the nearby village of Rangrik, which was probably destroyed in the 14th century when the Sakya sect rose to power with Mongol assistance. In the wake of the Chinese influence, it was rebuilt during the 14th century as an outstanding example of the monastic architecture.

In the 17th century, during the reign of the Fifth Dalai Lama, Key was attacked again by the Mongols and later became a Gelugpa establishment. In 1820, it was sacked again during the wars between Ladakh and Kullu.

In 1841, it was severely damaged by the Dogra army under Ghulam Khan and Rahim Khan. Later that same year it suffered more damage from a Sikh army.

In the 1840s, it was also ravaged by fire and in 1975 a violent earthquake caused more damage, which was repaired with the help of the Archaeological Survey of India and the State Public Works Department. The successive trails of destruction and patch-up jobs have resulted in a haphazard growth of box-like structures, and so the monastery looks like a fort, where temples are built on top of one another.

The walls of the monastery are covered by paintings and murals. It is an outstanding example of the monastic architecture, which developed during the 14th century in the wake of the Chinese influence.

Key monastery has a collection of ancient murals and books of high aesthetic value and it enshrines Buddha images and idols, in the position of Dhyana.

Monasteries in Dharamshala

Subsequent to the 14th Dalai Lama establishing his Tibetan exile government at Mcleod Ganj (a former colonial British summer picnic spot) near upper Dharamshala, the ancient Namgyal Monastery, which was first established by the third Dalai Lama in 1579 in Tibet, was relocated to Dharamshala (the district headquarters of the Kangra district), in 1959.

It is now the personal monastery of the Dalai Lama. Two hundred monks and young trainee monks reside here. They pursue studies of the major texts of Buddhist Sutras and Tantras, as also the Tibetan and English Languages.

Tsuglagkhang

An important Buddhist shrine (located opposite to the Namgyal Monastery in the same courtyard) in the town is the Tsuglagkhang or Tsuglag Khang, known as the Dalai Lama's temple. It houses the statues, in sitting postures, of Shakyamuni (gilded)- the central image, Avalokiteœvara (the deity of compassion sculpted in silver with eleven faces and thousand arms and eyes -linked to a legend), and Padmasambhava (Guru Rinpoche) – both facing the direction of Tibet – and also the Tibetan Institute of Performing Arts.

Dalai Lama's residence is opposite to this temple. A festival is held here every year, during April and May, when traditional dances and plays are enacted.8 kilometres (5.0 mi) away from Dharamshala, at Sidhpur, a small monastery called the Gompa Dip Tse-Chok Ling, the Gangchen Kyishong (called Gangkyi in short by Tibetans and Library by Indians is the premises of the Tibetan government-in-exile), Mani Lakhang Stupa, Nechung Monastery, Norbulingka Institute, Sidhpur are located. The Karmapa (who was in Norbulinga in Tibet before taking refuge in India) is now living in Gyato monastery.

Kalachakra Temple

Kalachakra Temple is located adjoining the Tsulagkhang which is dedicated to the Kalachakra. The temple has fresco decorations of 722 deities of the mandala, Shakayamuni Buddha, and the central Kalachakra image. Dalai Lama personally directed the painting of the frescos done by three master painters over a period of three years. The walls and columns here have many traditional Tibetan Thangka paintings.

Library of Tibetan works and archives

A Library of Tibetan Works and Archives (LTWA) was also set up by the Dalai Lama, in June 1970, to provide exhaustive information on Buddhist and Tibetan culture. The LTWA boasts of more than 110,000 titles in the form of manuscripts (40% are the Tibetan originals), books and documents; hundreds of thangkas (Tibetan scroll paintings), statues and other artefacts; and over 6,000 photographs, and many other materials.

The LTWA has nine departments guided by a governing body. The library conducts seminars, talks, meetings and discussions and also brings out an annual 'News Letter.' On the third floor of this library there is a museum (opened in 1974) that houses notable artefacts such as a three-dimensional carved wooden mandala of Avalokiteshvara and items that date back to the 12th century.

Norbulingka Institute

The Norbulingka Institute founded in 1988, by the present Dalai Lama has the primary objective of preserving the Tibetan language and cultural heritage.

This institute has been patterned on the same lines as Norbulingka, the traditional summer residence of the Dalai Lamas, in Lhasa, amidst a well-maintained garden setting, and the emphasis here is more on traditional art. A temple named as the "Seat of Happiness Temple" (Deden Tsuglakhang) is located here. Around this temple, craft centres are located, which specialise in traditional forms of Thanka painting to

Metal art that are considered integral to Tibetan Monastery architecture. 300 artisans work here and also impart training to their wards.

The Losel Doll Museum here has diorama displays of traditional Tibetan scenes, using miniature Tibetan dolls in traditional costumes.

A short distance from the institute lies the Dolma Ling Buddhist nunnery and the Gyato Monastery, temporary residence of the 17th Karmapa, Ogyen Trinley Dorje.

Festivals

Buddhist festivals held in Himachal Pradesh are predominantly connected with their religious identity. They relate to the seasons (New Year as per Lunar and Solar calendars), Buddha's birth and death anniversaries, and also the sacred days such as the birthdays of the Bodhistavas. The annual calendar is filled with festivals and some the popular ones starting with January are the following.

In January, in the Lahaul region, a carnival called the Halda Festival is held when people carry twigs of cedar tree to a location specified by the lamas and then throw it into a bonfire accompanied by various dances.

During February/March, the Tibetan New Year is observed as Losar festival by all Tibetan Buddhists in the state with processions, music and dancing; mask dances or chaam dances are popular on this occasion. The Dalai Lama holds teaching discourses at Dharmashala during this festival.

Ki Cham festival held in June/July is specific to Ki monastery. On this occasion, whirling mask dances are held in the monastery, which is watched by people from many villages of Spiti.

An ancient practice of a trade fair called the La Darcha is held in August in Spiti. Buddhist dances and Buddhist sports are popular and held along with rural marketing fair. Its social, economic and cultural significance relates to ancient ties with Tibet. Instead of La Darch ground near the Chicham village, the festival is now held at Kaza, headquarters of Spiti subdivision.

In November, the Guktor festival is held in Dhankar monastery in Spiti when processions and mask dances are the set festive practices.

In December, the International Himalayan Festival (a three-day event) is held in Mcleod Ganj, the exile capital of Tibet to celebrate the Dalai Lama getting the Noble Peace Prize. Dance and music mark the day with resolve to promote peace and cultural amity. On this occasion, the Dalai Lama blesses Mcleod Ganj.

9

Art, Architecture, Fair and Festivals

ARTS AND CRAFTS OF HIMACHAL PRADESH

Among arts and crafts that come out of Himachal Pradesh state in India are carpets, leather works, shawls, metalware, woodwork and paintings. Pashmina shawl is the product which is highly in demand not only in Himachal but all over the country. Colourful Himachali caps are also famous art work of the people. One tribe, *Dom*, is expert in manufacturing bamboo items like boxes, sofas, chairs, baskets and racks. Metalware of the state include utensils, ritualistic vessels, idols, gold and silverjewelleries.

Weaving, carving, painting, or chiselling is considered to be the part of the life of *Himachalis*. Himachal is well known for designing shawls, especially in Kullu. The architecture, objects, shops, museums, galleries and craftsmen charm with a variety perfected over time. Women take an active part in pottery and men in carpentry. For ages, wood has been used in Himachal in the construction of temples, homes, idols etc.

Weaving

The extreme winters of Himachal necessitated wool weaving. Nearly every household in Himachal owns a pit-loom. Wool is considered as pure and is used as a ritual cloth. The well known woven object is the shawl, ranging from fine pashmina to the coarse desar. Kullu is famous for its shawls with striking patterns and vibrant colors.

Himachali caps are of typical styles and they differ region to region. In Kinnaur, shawls, saris and trousers are woven in wool. The shawls woven in Rampur, known as Rampur chaddar, are known for their soft texture and durability. In Chamba district, weaving assumes a chequered pattern. Besides shawls, carpets and blankets are also a vital part of the Himachali lifestyle.

Wood craft

Himachal is the one of those areas in India where wood has played a significant role as a structural material. Pine, Cedrus deodara, walnut, horse chestnut and wild black mulberry are found in abundance in Himachal Pradesh. Places famous for woodcraft are Chamba, Tisza, Kalpa, Kinnaur district and Kullu. Village homes are constructed with carvings on doors, windows, balcony panels etc. This can be found in remote areas of the state, especially in the districts of Kinnaur and Kullu .

Metal craft

Objects crafted with metals fulfil the ritualistic needs of Himachalis. In 600 AD, the courts of the Himachali kings had mastered the craftsmen who were specialised in metalware. Antique metal statuettes are one of the most significant aspects in many temples of Himachal Pradesh. The statues of gods and goddesses also appear as *mohras* or in metal plaques.

In fact, metalcraft in the state grew around temples and palaces. Repousse technique was made in use to create the temple doors of *Vajreshwari Devi*, *Jwalamukhi* in Kangra, *Bhimkali* in Sarahan and *Chandika Devi* in Kinnaur district.

A canopy made of gold at the Jwalamukhi temple is one of the example of Himachal's metalwork which believed to have been gifted by Mughal emperor Akbar the Great. The metalwork of Kinnaur depicts a unique synthesis of Buddhism and Hinduism.

Brass is often used for trending household utensils. Some of the towns where good metal work is found are Bilaspur, Chamba, Reckong Peo, Rohru, Sarahan and Jogindernagar.

ARTS & CRAFT

Photo: Jewellery Work, Himachal Pradesh

The arts and crafts of any region are a reflection of its environment, people and traditions. So it is in Himachal. Weaving, as carving , painting, or chiselling – are such an intrinsic part of the Himachal life! The scenic beauty of the region transfers into the creations, as it were, and the result is colourful pashminas, exquisite wooden doors, rhythmic sculptures. From the upper reaches of Lahaul and Spiti down to the lowlands of Kangra – life and its shades are woven in, painted on, felt in soulful rhythms or celebrated with joyous abandon, carved in, engraved... whether it is the miniature paintings of Kangra, the thangka artefacts of Spiti, or the beautiful shawls of Kullu. As you move through the state, an enchanting and colourful tapestry unfolds – the architecture, objects, shops, museums, galleries and craftsmen charm with the variety and mastermanship perfected through the ages. If you happen to be in Kangra town, walk into the narrow winding lane called Kumhar Gali, linked to the bazaar leading to the Kangra Devi temple in the heart of the town. You will find a row of double storeyed houses surrounded by large courtyards and entire families bent over potters‘ wheels, beating the clay or applying a coat to the finished pots.

While women take an active part in pottery, when it comes to carpentry, it is an exclusive male domain. For centuries, wood has been used in Himachal in the construction and ornamentation of temples, homes, idols and so on. The skill is hereditary and is passed on from father to son. The master wood carver of Chamba, Malik Lateef, for example, belongs to a family of traditional carpenters. His father Ali Baksh worked in the courts of the Chamba king and his artefacts are still preserved in the Bhuri Singh Museum in Chamba. The districts where you are likely to find the most exquisite woodcraft are Chamba, Kulu, Mandi, Mahasua and Bilaspur

FAMOUS ART & CRAFTS

Woven Craft

It is the extreme cold winters of Himachal that necessitated wool weaving. Almost every household in Himachal owns a pit-loom and it is not unusual to find men and women spinning yarn on a spindle walking down the roads of Himachali villages. Wool is also regarded as pure and is used as a ritual cloth. The best-known woven object is the shawl, ranging from extremely fine pashmina to the coarse desar. Kullu in particular has been famous for its shawls with striking geometrical patterns and vibrant colours – the distinctive feature being stripes running along the edges.

Himachali topis or caps are of distinctive styles and are different for every region. In Kinnaur, not only shawls, but also saris, trousers and pyjamas are woven in wool. The shawls woven in Rampur, known as Rampur chaddar, are famous for their soft texture and durability. In Chamba district, the weaving assumes a chequered pattern. Besides shawls, carpets and blankets are an essential part of the Himachali lifestyle. Carpets in brilliant colours are woven with a variety of traditional motifs – there are garudas on flowering trees, dragons, swastikas, flutes symbolising happiness or lotus blooms signifying purity. Carpets are woven as furnishing, as saddles for horses and as blankets or chutkas. They are also a part of every bride's trousseau.

Wood Craft

Himachal is the only area in India, besides Kerala, where wood has played an important role as a structural material. The most abundant wood in Himachal's forests is the pine and deodar, besides walnut, horse chestnut and wild black mulberry. Villages famous for woodcraft are Chamba, Chhatrarhi, Brahmaur, Koonr, Tisa (Chamba); Kalpa, Thangi, Rarang, Sapni, Batseri, Shaung, Bari and Bhaba (Kinnaur); Dungri, Banjar and Saraj (Kullu). Earliest wooden temples in Himachal date as far back as sixth century AD and are located in Brahmaur and Chhatrarhi in Chamba. Many other temples sculpted in wood lie scattered all over Himachal. Village homes too are extensively ornamented with carvings – on doors, windows, balcony panels etc – some exquisite examples may be found in villages as remote as Kamru, Sangla, Chitkul, villages in Kinnaur and Jagatsukh, Vashishta and villages around Manali and Kullu. The craft also translates into wooden idols of gods and goddesses in classical as well as rural styles. Utilitarian objects crafted in wood can be often found in Pahari homes – these may include rectangular boxes to store grains or ornaments: the extent of carving indicates the social strata of its owner.

The Gaddi households in Chamba and Brahmaur were famous for their attractive wooden utensils. Kinnauri villages still use wooden household utensils extensively. The nobility in the state brought in European influences and employed craftsmen to create chairs, tables, cabinets, picture frames, cigar boxes, screens, walking sticks etc. Wood is used in rituals by way of temple chariots, low settees, sandals, wooden pipes etc. Intricately carved wooden spinning wheels were used in the past – the ornamentation has faded of late. However, at large, wodcarving is still a living tradition in Himachal.

Metalcraft

Objects crafted with metal fulfil religious, ritualistic and everyday needs of the people of Himachal. Even in AD 600, the courts of the Himachali kings had master craftsmen who specialised in metalware, and antique metal statuettes are a feature in many temples of the state. There are fine examples of freestanding metal statues at temple entrances in Brahmaur, Chamba and the Vajreshwari Devi temple in Kangra. Gods and goddesses also appear as mohras or in metal plaques – which are used during processions and festivals. In fact, metalcraft in Himachal grew around temples and palaces. Repousse technique was used to create beautiful temple doors – temples of Vajreshwari Devi, Jwalamukhi in Kangra, Bhimkali in Sarahan and Chandika Devi in Kinnaur employ this technique to perfection. Bronze figurines, particularly that of goddess Durga killing the demon Mahisha is a common sight in most households. Low settees made of silver or brass are another common ritual artefact used in homes as well as temples, besides bells, incense burners, lamps, jars, flasks, tridents, fly whisks, and canopies.

A famous canopy made of gold is the one at the Jwalamukhi temple, believed to have been gifted by emperor Akbar. The metal artefacts of Kinnaur represent a unique synthesis of Buddhism and Hinduism. There are ritual cups, daggers, kettles, jugs, prayer wheels, conch trumpets and so on. Brass is often used in the hills for fashioning household utensils. The Kinnaur metalsmiths also specialise in the repousse worked door handles fashioned in the form of crocodile, dragon or lion-head. All sacred buildings display these handles. Another interesting item is the dongbo or tea churner, as common as the intricately carved hookah bases in these parts. Some of the towns where good metal work may be found are Bilaspur, Chamba, Kupa, Rekong Peo, Rohru, Sarahan and Jogindernagar.

Jewellery

Pahari jewellery is artistic and elaborate. It has the vigour and sturdiness of style that comes from nature itself. The designs are borrowed from simple motifs like seeds, flowers and leaves and developed into exquisite patterns. While different communities wear jewellery unique to their traditions, some ornaments are worn all over.

These include the hemispherical boss or chak – worn on the crown and both sides of the head. Neck ornaments are important in all districts – from collar like hansli or small pendants called toke.

The Pahari variant of the torque is a long necklace of numerous chains linked together by silver plaques. Chandanhaar is a necklace comprising five or seven rows of facetted gold beads. One of the most cherished neckpieces is a coin necklace. The choker worn here is called kach and consists of silver beads and triangular plaques. Earrings are often worn with drops or granulations, nose studs are embedded with precious and semiprecious stones and often, an ornament of pendants is strung to it. Chiri tikka is a flat piece of silver, enamelled or embedded with pearls and suspended from the centre of the forehead while several chains hang along the hairline on both sides.

The jutti is a heavy bunch of silver tassels or flowers, attached to the plait while a smaller ornament, beshtar is tied to the plait ends. Men, women and children often wear silver amulets to ward off evil spirits – a tradition carried to the hills from the plains. In lower Himachal, there is a marked preference for gold ornaments while deeper in the villages, silver is more common. While there is a basic homogeneity in the jewellery and style of adornment, each community has ornaments distinct to it. Some important towns for buying hill jewellery are Moti Bazaar in Mandi, Chaugan bazaar in Chamba, Kangra town, Sultanpur and Kullu. There is also a village called Sunarion ki Gaon near Rohru, where many families are engaged in jewellery fashioning.

FAIRS & FESTIVALS OF HIMACHAL PRADESH INDIA

Himachal Pradesh is a land of cultural diaspora! Words fail to define the mixture of different cultures. For the people of Himachal Pradesh, every day is nothing less than a celebration or jubilation. The festivals vary in terms of scale but most of them are attended by huge crowds who want to carry forward the rich legacy and rituals of their ancestors.

Every monastery, temple, church, gurudwara stages its own celebration, featuring parades of deities in gleaming golden silver canopies, performance of traditional dances like mask dance, thrilling adventure activities and ritual dramas. In Himachal Pradesh, every festival is celebrated in peace or by dancing the hours away in carefree abandonment. There are so many cultural festivals in Himachal Pradesh that it is really hard to pick some.

Halda festival – Welcome the New Year

Dedicated to the goddess of wealth, Shashikar Apa, Halda festival is celebrated with great zeal and enthusiasm in order to celebrate the new year. The actual date of the celebration is decided by the Lamas. People of Lahaul districts come together and enjoy their new year by performing music.

Lamas also choose a different site to execute an old ritual as per which, every household carries few branches of a cedar tree to perform a bonfire. The bonfire signifies the unity of the community. It is more popular in the valleys of Keylong, River Chandra and River Bhaga.

- When: January
- Where: Lahaul district
- Special Attraction: Dancing Acts, Musicals
- Duration of Festival: 2 Days

Sazo

The most awaited festival of Himachal Pradesh, Sazo is celebrated to bid adieu to the village deities. During the festival, the doors of the temples remain closed, but the wagons of god and goddesses remain open. It is believed that on this day, various deities abode to heaven for a short nap. The ritual signifies that God showers good things from heaven on its devotees. Therefore, the village people clean and polish the floors of the temples to receive God's blessings. Throughout the festival, villagers are filled with joy and ecstasy.

On this day, priests of the temples are deeply revered as they are considered as the representative of the deity. In some villages, priests of the temple go from one house to another just to sniff the incense. Villages give the priest a cordial reception; as a regard they also gift them food grains and gifts, a small ritual known as the Deacher and Deokhel. Poltus, Rice, Pulses, Vegetables, Meat, Halva, Chilta are some of the dishes prepared by the villagers on this occasion.

- When: January
- Where: Kinnaur
- Special Attraction: Dancing Acts, Musicals
- Duration of Festival: 1 Day

Lohri /Maghi

Lohri is a feisty festival celebrated by the people of Himachal Pradesh, Haryana and Punjab. In the villages of Punjab, Lohri is celebrated as a ceremonial ritual to jumpstart the harvesting of Rabi crop. Lohri festival is famous by the name of Maghu as well because it coincides with the onset of 'Magh' month which commences just a day before.

On this festival, people dress in vibrant clothes and prepare dance performances. Children sing folk songs and go door to door, especially to the newly married couples consciously to collect funds for community bonfire. Around dusk, people from different households come together and lit a bonfire. People throw pop cans and puffed rice in the flames as a way of offering sacrifice to God so that they get blessed with a rich harvest. People from different communities come together for the grand holy celebration. On the whole, Lohri celebrates oneness and encourages people to rise above personal differences.

- When: 13th January
- Where: All over Himachal
- Special Attraction: Bonfire, dancing acts
- Duration of Festival: 1 Day

Himachal Winter Carnival

To promote the culture of Himachal Pradesh, a winter carnival is organized every year in Manali. Himachal Pradesh started the trend of Winter Carnival back in 1977 and now after almost three decades the festival has become bigger and better! During this festival, the ski slopes of Manali are invaded by adventure enthusiasts. Another major highlight of the festival is the beauty contest known as the "Winter Queen" and "Mr. Manali"

A procession is also organized from the Hadimba Devi temple. The complete stretch of Manali mall road looks like a carnival. Right from folk dance to entertaining skits, a lot of things can be explored in this festival. People on a tour to Himachal Pradesh can't afford to miss the Himachal Winter Carnival. Other than enjoying the Himachal Winter Carnival in Manali, tourists have an opportunity to visit The Manacle Gompa, Vashisht Springs, Jagatsukh, Manu Temple and Hadimba Temple.

- When: 2nd January to 6th January
- Where: Manali
- Special Attraction: Skiing Championship, Himachali Food Festival, Craft Bazaar, Local Band Competition, Folk Dances, Street Plays, and Adventure Sports.
- Duration of Festival: 1 Day

Losar Festival

The New Year celebration of Tibetans, Losar festivals takes place in the first week of the first lunar month (February), with performances of Tibetan opera and prayer ceremonies being held at various monasteries. A day prior to the New Year, Nyi Shu GU is celebrated which is a ritualistic tradition. Special noodles called Thukpa Bhatuk are consumed on this day (Nyi Shu GU). During this festival, the local deity is worshipped. It is also believed that the Losar festival originated during the Pre-Buddhist period in Tibet when Bon was the religion followed in the country.

The First day of the festival is known as the 'Lama Losar' or the festival of the Guru and His Holiness The Dalai Lama', the spiritual head of the Tibetans is worshiped on this day. During the festival, Chaam dance is performed which features elaborated mask and costumes. The dance presents the story of how the cruel Tibetan king, known by the name of Langdarma, was killed in the 9th century, leading to the ultimate triumph of good over evil. The weird masks used in the dance have also earned it the name the 'Devil Dance'.

- When: Between the months of January end and March
- Where: Throughout Himachal
- Special Attraction: Mask Dance
- Duration of Festival: 15 days

Doongri Festival, Kullu

Doongri festival or Hadimba Devi fair is celebrated in Kullu in honor of and to celebrate Hadimba Devi's (wife of Bhima) birthday. A huge fair is organized on this day; during the festival one can catch glimpses of dance and musical performances by local artists. Since the festival is celebrated on 'Basant Panchami', one can see colourful flowers blooming on Kullu valley. Moreover, little colorful kites also cover the skies to mark the spring festival, termed as "Basant Panchami." Freshness, aroma, and vibrancy of flowers all around the valley gives the tourist the most blissful time of their lives.

- When: May
- Where: Kullu
- Special Attraction: Folk dance and music performances by the local artist
- Duration of Festival: 1 Day

Maha Shivaratri

Maha Shivratri is celebrated in the month of February with great zeal and enthusiasm. Shivratri was the day when Lord Shiva married Goddess Parvati. Maha Shivaratri literally means 'The Night of Shiva.' All the religious ceremonies and celebrations take place during the night. During the daytime, people make sculptures of the main deity Shiva and Parvati with the help of cow dung or earthen soil. A 3 day fair called Mandi International Maha Shivratri Festival is organized in Mandi, a small town of Himachal Pradesh.

- When: February or March
- Where: Throughout Himachal
- Special Attraction: Folk music, dance, trade of general commodities
- Duration of Festival: 1 Day

Mandi Shivaratri Fair

A grand celebration called International Maha Shivratri Festival is organized by Mandi. Since the temple is home to 81 temples of Lord Shiv, Mandi sees footfall of more than 200 devotees on the day of Shivratri. The festival is also known as a Mandi Shivratri festival. During the festival, a colorful procession called Shobha Yatra is organized as per which various deities are carried in their chariots to Mandi to pay homage to Madho Rai and the Raja. As per the old ritual, it is mandatory that every deity who visits Mandi should visit Madho Rai temple first in order to pay respect to Lord Vishnu and then honor the ruler. Consequently, the deity pays obeisance to Lord Shiv at Bhootnath temple where the main festival is organized. The entire procession is swayed by drums and folk music to indicate happiness.

Shivratri is the time when local businessman indulge in trading activities of products like walnut, ghee (butter oil), honey opium and general merchandise. On the second day, Jagaran is organized. On this occasion, a guru and his disciple make prophesies for the following year. On the last day, prayers are chanted and 'chadars' are offered in the temple.

- When: February or March
- Where: Mandi
- Special Attraction: Folk music, dance, trade of general commodities
- Duration of Festival: 3 Days

Nalwari Fair

Celebrated with great pomp and show since colonial times, Nalwari fair is a great platform for all the cattle traders to meet and do business. The festival was started by W. Goldstein, who was the superintendent of Shimla in 1889. He was so impressed with the breed of cattle produced in Himchal Pradesh that he decided to organize a fair where cattle could be bought and sold here.

The prime attraction of the Nalwari Festival is the Bullock trade. This week long festival attracts traders, business men and tourist from all across India. Nalwari Festival is the time when shopaholics can grab some interesting local artifacts like jewelry, paintings and local folk art. A wrestling match is also organized during the festival.

- When: 17th March to 23rd March
- Where: Bilaspur
- Special Attractions: Wrestling Match, Musical Events, Shopping of local art, Cattle trading
- Duration of Festival: 7 Days

Baisakh/ Vaisakhi

Baisakh or Vaisakhi is marked as the end of the winter season as per the agrarian tradition. The festival is celebrated with great pomp and show in Rewalsar, Prashar Lake near

Mandi and Tattapanii near Shimla. Fairs are organized in every nook and corner of Himachal Pradesh. Wrestling, dancing and archery competitions are the main attractions of the festival.

In Kangra, a small clay model of Rali is made in every house to mark the day. Fairs by different names are organized in various places of Himachal Pradesh- Sui Mela in Chamba, Maha Naug Festival in Mandi, Markandaya fair in Bilaspur, and Rohru Jatra in Shikhru.

- Where: All across Himachal Pradesh
- When 13th or 14th of April
- Special Attraction: Baisakhi fair, folk dance performances; Wrestling, archery and dancing competition
- Duration of Festival: 1 Day

Spring Festival

Spring festival, which is also called Pipal Jatra or Basantotsav, takes place in Kullu from 28th to 30th April. The tradition of celebrating the festival began long back when kings used to rule Himachal Pradesh. The festival marks the beginning of the spring season in the valley. It is said that during the bygone era, rulers used to sit under the papal tree to enjoy the traditional dances. As the time rolled by, the festival has lost much of its glory and glitters. During the festival, cultural performances are organized by Kala Kendra in amphitheatres. Cultural groups and reputed artists come from all over India to perform in the festival.

- Where: Kullu
- When: 28th to 30th April
- Special Attractions: Cultural performances
- Duration of Festival: 3 Days

Rakhidumni (Rakhi) Festival

Rakhidumni or Rakhi is celebrated on the full moon day in the monsoon month of Bhadrapad. The festival is celebrated to acknowledge the emotional bond of brother and sister. On this day, every sister ties a thread on her brother's writs, which acts as a bond of protection. Rakhi signifies that a brother will protect his sister from all the evil of the world. The sacred thread remains on the wrist of the brothers for the entire month and when the Sairi festival comes, threads are removed and offered to Mother Sairi.

On this day, sisters pray for the long life of their brothers. In many parts of Himachal Pradesh, Rakhi is known by the name Kajri Navami or Kajri Purnima. This is the time when Goddess Bhagwati is worshipped. The festival is also known by different names-Vish Tarak (destroyer of Venom), Punya Pradayak (bestower of boons) and Pap Nashak (the destroyer of sins). This is the time when all the people of the family come together and share a good time with each other.

- Where: All across Himachal Pradesh.
- When: August or September
- Duration of Festival: 1 Day

Phulaich Festival

Phulaich means 'the festival of flowers' and as per Hindu calendar it is organized in the month of Bhadrapada. The festival is associated with the blooming of flowers in the Kinnaur valley.

On this day, local villagers go to the mountains to collect Ladra flowers swayed by playing drums. The festival is organized as an act of remembering the ones passed away. Relatives offer rice, wine and food to the deceased ones, which later are distributed amongst the poor. Later, villagers go to visit the Dhangaspa family house and show their respect by garlanding the members of the family. A true reflection of Hilly culture can be seen in the colourful celebration process.

- When: September
- Where: Kinnaur
- Special Attraction: Cultural practices
- Duration of Festival: 7 Days

Ladarcha Festival / La Darcha Fair

If tourists want to catch the glimpses of vibrant hilly culture of Himachal Pradesh then they should attend the La Darch festival. The festival is organized to strengthen the commercial bond between India and Tibet. The fair attracts many regional traders, local inhabitants, and tourist from across the world. The festival was abandoned in the year 1962 because of China war, but it was started again in the year 1980. The main attraction of the festival are folk song and dance performances by artists from the Tibetan Institute of Performing Art, Bhutan, Ladakh, Sikkim, Kinnaur and Nepal.

Traders from Kullu, Lahaul and Kinnaur districts gather here during this festival. Many items are traded like accessories, utensils, apparel, jewelry, metalwork, plastic goods, craft, dry fruits, grains and even livestock- yaks and pure blood horses. The festival is organized with a purpose to promote friendship and cultural understanding amongst the people living in Himalayan region.

Special attractions of the festival are Chaam and Buchan dance, special Buddhist sermons and archery competition. The calm and serene valley of Kaza is transformed into a bustling carnival during the festival.

- When: 3rd week of August
- Where: Kaza, Spiti
- Special Attraction: Folk dance, cultural programmes, special Buddhist sermons (large community meals)
- Duration of Festival: 3 Days

Kullu Dussehra

Dussehra celebration in Kullu is not at all similar to celebration in other parts of the country as no figurine of Ravan or Kumbhkarna is burned. The traditional Kullu Dussehra is organized in the month of October and gets off a spectacular start with the traditional procession of Lord Raghunathji. The Rath Yatra of the idol of Lord Ragunath is led by the Kullu Raja and village deities, and is known as the running of the

Gods. Lord Raghunathji saddled on a gaily attired chariot is pulled from its fixed place in Dhalpur Maidan to another spot across the Maidan by big ropes. The pulling of ropes is regarded sacred by the local people. All the deities from various temples are brought from the temple to the foreground in order to pay homage to Raghnathji. Here one can see one of the most spectacular processions in the country as well as the state; it attracts a huge number of tourists.

Celebration commences on 'Vijaya Dashmi' day; over 250 people gather here and camp at Dhalpur Maidan for a week in order to pay obeisance to Lord Raghunathji, the presiding deity. The festival is celebrated with complete fevours for a week. This Hindu festival is celebrated all over India to mark the triumph of good over evil (Lord Ram over Ravan). On the last day of the festival, the chariot of Raghunath ji is taken to the bank of the river Beas. Then a heap of wood along with grass is set on fire, symbolizing the burning of effigies of Ravana, the demon of Lanka, and is followed by the sacrifice of chosen animals.

- Where: Kullu
- When: November or October
- Special Attraction:
- Duration of Festival: 1 Day

International Himalayan Festival

The international Himalayan festival is celebrated in the Kangra district of Himachal Pradesh to commemorate the occasion when His Holiness The Dalai Lama was awarded Nobel Peace prize in the year 1985. The festival holds a special significance as it symbolizes the peace initiative. Indo-Tibetan Friendship Society along with the Central Tibetan Administration and Himachal Pradesh Tourism sponsors the Global Himalayan Festival.

International Himalayan Festival lasts for three days in McLeodganj. Different stalls in the festival showcase the culture, handicrafts, traditional medicines, and cuisines of the Himalayan region. The festival acts as an initiative to strengthen harmony between the inhabitants of Himachal Pradesh and Tibetans.

- When: 2nd week of December
- Where: Kangra valley
- Special Attractions: Ctural Programmes, Art
- Duration of Festival: 3 Days

Ice Skating Carnival

To one's astonishment, Shimla is home to the biggest natural ice skating rink in Asia. That is why it is just the right place to host Ice Skating Carnival. Being in close proximity to Pierre Panjar, Dhauladar, Shivalik and Himalayas, the city is blessed with the perfect weather to conduct full-fledged winter sports for visiting tourists. Ice Skating Carnival is a managed by the Skating club of Shimla, which has been successfully running the program for over 60 years. The carnival is celebrated with a lot of pomp and splendour in Himachal Pradesh and has a huge influx of visitors each year.

Ice-skating, skiing, figure skating, chain tags, speed hockey and ice hockey are some of the prominent sports which can be played here. Other than sports, various recreational activities like fancy dress and dance competition are organized side by side.

- Where: Dalhousie or Shimla
- When: From December to February
- Special Attraction:
- Duration of Festival: 3 Months

FAIRS IN HIMACHAL, HIMACHAL PRADESH FAIRS

There are 20 state level fairs or festivals recognised by the the Government at present in Himachal Pradesh. They have an educational, social as well as religious character. These serve the needs of social integration not only for economic sustenance but also for cultural survival. Generally the fairs are held at such a time when the people are free from their household engagements. Fairs give them an opportunity to purchase and sell needed articles. Traders from far and near join these festivals to display articles like clothes, wool, pashmina, furs, leather, hides and skins, pottery, metal ware, jewellery, ornaments, fruits, vegetables and many other local products coming from the homes and fields of the ruralities.Fairs in Himachal Pradesh have very positive role to play in social life. Himachal is a land of Devi and Devtas - land of gods and most of the fairs are of mythological nature. But to keep on rhythm in various walks of life, fairs have occupied predominant role and aquired varied dimensions, such as trade, agricultural, seasonal and fairs connected with festivals etc. So intensive the fairs hava become, that people of all shades and interests participate in large numbers. There is hardly any village where no fair is held. There is almost continuous succession of fairs.

Baisakhi

This fair is held at various places in the state. People carry village deity with music procession from one place to another. In upper hills, people perform 'Mala Dance' by joining hands to form a large circle. During day time, some games like archery and wrestling are also played.

Minjar Fair (Chamba)

This festival is held in the month of August on second Sunday. It continues for a week. Minjar (maize flowers) festival is celebrated in district Chamba at a place 'Chowgan' in Chamba town.Maize flowers, a coconut, a rupee or a smaller coin, a fruit and a few paddy tentacles are offered to Varuna, the god of rain. It is a state fair. It is difficult to say, when the fair first started, but the present form of the fair is attributed to Raja Sahil Verman, who ruled the state in the 10th century A.D.

Naina Devi Fair

This fair is held in the month of August, at Naina Devi Temple, in district Blaspur, which is 8 km. from the Gangul Power House. This is the most delightful fair in district Bilaspur.

Kullu Dushehra

Kullu Dushehra mirrors Himachal culture in its entirely.. It clearly shows the lefestyle, love of dance and music of the people in this region. To see the colorful Himachal at one place, Kullu Dushehra is the right place. Although Dushehra is celebrated all over the country, but in Kullu, it has its own distinctive glamour. This is a state fair.People from Punjab, Haryana, Delhi and Uttar Pradesh throng to enjoy Kullu Dushehra.

Lavi Fair

This fair is held in the month of October or November every at Rampur Bushahr. In ancient, Tibet and Kinnaur had good trade relations and Lavi fair is the outcome of business interest of both sides. People from other areas in general and tribal belt in particular participate in this fair with horses, mules, pashminas, colts, yaks, chilgoza, namdas, pattis, woollens, raw semi-finished wool and other dry fruits produced in the state are brought for selling. It is three hundred years old fair and also a state fair.4 During day time, hectic trade activities are witnessed all over the town. At night, folks dances and music around small bonfires are organised. It continues for three days.

Chrewal

It is also known as Prithvi pooja in some places. It is celebrated on the Ist of Bhadon - middle of August. This continues for full one month. The farmers do not yoke oxen during this month. In Kullu, this festival is known as Badranjo. In Chamba, it is called Pathroru. It is a festival of flowers here. This is an occasion of great celebration, particularly for girls who dance on this day.

Renuka Fair

This fair is celebrated in the month of November for six days in district Sirmaur. It starts ten days after the famous

Diwali festival. The legend goes that Parshuram, the youngest son of mother Renuka, used to visit his mother every year.

The fair commemorates the annual meeting of Parshuram and Renuka. Parshuram is believed to be the sixth incarnation of Lord Vishnu.

One can see the glimpses of hill culture at the fair. Rural people market their produce of walnuts, dried and wet ginger ect.

Folk dances, magic show, Kariyala play, thoda dance, wrestling bouts, fire works, police and homeguard's band display, developmental exhibitions, cinema shows and bhajan-kirtan are other attractions of the week long fair. It is a state fair.

Shivratri Fair

This fair is held in the month of February on Shivratri day in Mandi. Shiva is the chief deity of Himachal Pradesh. This festival is given the greatest importance even in temples all through Himachal Pradesh. This fair continues for a week, with great fun and frolic.On this occasion people bring hundreds of Gods and Goddesses in their Raths. Devotees carry them on shoulders amidst melodious religious songs. People pay their homage to Lord Shiva at famous temple of Bhut Nath in Mandi town. It is a state fair.

Holi Fair

It is held in the month of March every year. Especially the Holi Mela of Sujanpur in district Hamirpur is very famous. It is the festival of colors. People all over Himachal come to participate in it. A week long fair provides wholesome entertainment through various games, songs, dances, folk dramas and skits performed by local artists/ Business activities are also in full swing throughout the week.

Chintpurni Fair

It is locally known as Mata-Da-Mela (fair of mother goddess). It is held in the village Chintpurni near Bharwain (a hill station on Hoshiarpur-Kangra road in Una district). According to one legend a certain Mai Das had the first darshan of the Mother goddess who appeared to him as a girl and asked him to perform the Pooja (worship) of the Pindi (idol) of the mother.

Henceforth generation after generation, the mother has promised to ward off the worldly worries and anxieties of those worshipping her. On the 8th day during Navratras the offering of Karahi (sweet halwa prasad) and Chhattar are made by the devotees.

The Nalwari Fair

This fair is held in the month of march every year. The idea of this fair was conceived by W. Goldstein.

He was the Superintendent of Shimla Hill States in 1889. The idea was motivated by a shortage of the good breed cattle, especiaaly bullocks. Now this fair has become more a business opportunity event. It is a state fair.

Sissu Fair

Sissu is a common fair celebrated all over the Buddhist Himalayas. Its main attraction is always a masked dance but because of a part of monastic rituals, it is always staged inside the monastery on the attached courtyard. The fair is celebrated on different dates at different places. At Sissur Gompa it is held in June, at Gemur Gompa in July and at Mani Gompa of Gondhla in August.

Lohri

In some areas, it is also known as Maghi or Saza. It is celebrated on the Ist of Magh - mid January. People celebrate it more as a continuation of the season of festivals. After finishing agricultural activities, they feast and celebrate and avail themselves of the time to meet their relatives. This festival continues for 8 days. On 8th day, people make get together and show social solidarity. Dance and music goes on for the whole night.

Bharmaur Jatra Fair

It is held in district Chamba in the month of August. There is a very colorful crowd in this fair.

Chhitrari Jatra Fair

It is held in district Chamba in the month of September. It is a very famous one day fair and a large number of prople gather in this fair from near and far.

Sui Fair

It is held in Chamba town in the month of April. This fair is exclusively for women. There is a temple of Naina Devi where women gather and worship the Devi. Naina was the queen of Raja Sahil Verman. This temple has been constructed at a place where she had sacrificed herself to bring water to Chamba town.

Tara Devi Fair

Durga Devi's temple of Taradevi is located on the ridge of mountain about 8 km. away from Shimla town. The fair is held here on Ashtami in Navratras os Asawin - September or October. This is called Durga Ashtami. A lot of tourists do visit it for its scenic beauty and worship of the famous mother goddess.

Jwalamukhi Fair

The Jwalamukhi fair is held twice a year during Navratras for worship of Durga goddess. It is the most imporatant fair in the Kangra valley. People come with red silken flags (dhwaja) to greet the Mother Goddess. The fair is attributed to the worship of that Eternal Flame which is coming out of earth spontaneously and perpetually.

Dal Fair

It is held on the bank of lake Dal, in the month of August in district Kangra at Dharamshala. This area is also ideal for a day picnic.

Nalwari Fair

It is held in district Kullu at Manali in the month of May. It is a very famous fair and a large number of prople gather in this fair from near and far.

Dungri Fair

It is held in district Kullu at Manali in the month of May.

Sarshi Jatra Fair

In district Kullu, at place Naggar in the month of May.

Banjar Fair

In district Kullu in the month of Mat and June.

Markanda Fair

In district Bilaspur at place Markanda in the month of April.

Solan Fair

Solan fair is held in the last week of June for three days. This fair is celebrated even before the present Solan town was founded in honour of the goddess 'Shulini' whose temple is situated in the nearby village named Solan Gaon. It attracts traders, sweetsellers, general merchants and other shopkeepers to make brisk business. The highlight of this fair are dancing, singing and wrestling.

Sari Fair

It is held in district Solan at town 'Arki in the month of July. This fair is famous for bull fighting.

Buffalo Fair

In district Shimla at village Kufri near Mashobra in the month of September.

Sipi Fair

In district Shimla near Mashobra in the month of May.

Jatar Rohru Fair

In district Shimla at Rohru town in the month os April.

Rampuri Jatar

In district Shimla at village Rampuri near Jubbal town in the month of July.

Thalog Fair

This fair is held in the honour of Devta Rahatna whose temples are located at Thalog and Jabna.

It is held at the end of Baishkha, in Prgana Jakholi of Chopal. It is 13 km. away from Chamba. The game archery, numerous sweet shops and Jhula are the main attractions like other fairs.

Trilokpur Fair

In district Sirmaur at village Trilokpur near Nahan town, in the month of September.

Phul Yatra Fair

Phul Yatra fair is held in Pangi at Killar in 'Asoj' every year. It denotes the start of a closing season in this snow bound valley.

Offerings are made to local goddess, in whose honour it is celebrated. The tribal people enjoy, dance, sing and drink in gay mood forgetting everything else for the time being.

In Kinnaur and Lahaul-Spiti some annuar fairs are held which have left deep impression on the community life of the tribals. One of the main features of these fairs is folk dance. Mask dance and lion dance are also very famous.

Sayar Fair

It is a famous fair observed in the month of September at a number of places such as Bakloh in Kangra, Karsog in Mandi, and Subathu in Shimla.

WOODEN ART AND ARCHITECTURE OF HIMACHAL PRADESH

A wooden temple is a subtle reproduction of a deodar tree in form and spirit. If nature has bestowed deodar tree to conceptualize a temple, the man has contributed his artistic talent, ingenuity and skill to make it beautiful. Thus, a wooden temple identifies itself with the divine wood, not only materially and externally, but spiritually and internally also, and if deodar is divine wood, the edifice made out of it is divine abode. (Handa 2006:81)

Temples made in wood are peculiar to this region, where the myriad patterns of woodwork on different elements of these temples is striking, wood figuring either as the primary raw material or in combination with stone. The earliest surviving wooden temples in the state of Himachal Pradesh are the classical structures built after the seventh century, the most famous of which are the Lakshana Devi Temple at Bharmaur, the Mrikula Devi Temple at Udaipur, the Shakti Devi Temple complex at Chhattrari, and the Dakshineshwar Mahadeva Temple at Nirmand.

That there existed some religious structural activity prior to these classical monuments is confirmed by the horde of precious coins belonging to the Trigarta and Audumbara rulers dating back to the second century BCE, collected from sites in districts of Kangra and Pathankot. These coin findings by colonial surveyors like Alexander Cunningham and Vincent A. Smith, and Indian historians such as Rakhal Das Banerjee depict illustrations of temple-like timber structures of simple execution, with single and multi-storied superstructures on wooden pillars, often accompanied with a circumambulatory passage around the structure.

Diversely identified by scholars owing to their different architectural traits, these illustrations on the coins could either be representations of multi-storied stupas or of temples: coins depict both domical and pointed-roof superstructures. The most perplexing of these depicts a small dome resting on flat roof held up by numerous pillars, with a figure of a trident with an axe on the side. This emblem clearly indicated affiliation to Shaivism, the domical feature perhaps a borrowing from Buddhist traditions. Most of the coins, however, depict temple structures with much in common with the present religious monuments in the region. Existing temples in the region, both stone and wooden, seem to be a more developed form of the illustrated temples. The single-storied pointed roofed forms are now termed pent-roofed temples; multi-storied structures correspond to the pagoda type; and the typical *nágara* temples of the north Indian type are derivations of the domical roofs in the coin illustrations.

Elaborating on these 'hill' temple styles helps understand how and where wood is utilized highlighting its significance in construction and the building of religious monuments of the region. The first type, the *na gara* temples, are largely stone structures with curvilinear conical superstructures, often accompanied with a wooden *manòdòapa*, as in case of the Champavati temple at Chamba.

Fig. : Lakshana Devi Temple, Bharmour

The pent-roofed temples are indigenously styled circular or rectangular structures with slanting roofs made of rows and rows of slates, designed, in keeping with the climatic conditions of the region, to keep heavy rainfall and snowfall from covering these structures for more than short intervals. An interesting feature very specific to these hill temples is the peculiar arrangement of wood and stone in building the walls. Wooden beams are laid at right angles of the walls, and intervening spaces are filled up with stone which holds itself quite beautifully protecting the inmates from harsh climatic conditions. Woodcarving on the façade on such temples, especially on the doorframe is striking. An odd number of receding jambs and lintels intricately carved with a variety of patterns decorate the doorframes. Another wood-carved part of the complex is the ceiling, usually following the 'lantern' style with detailed wooden sculpting (floral patterns or religious themes) on geometric patterns, the final effect being quite mesmerising.

Pagoda temples are similar to the abovementioned pent-roofed temples in plan and style. The difference lies in the superstructure: these are multi-storied varying from two to five. Each superimposed story is slightly smaller than the one below forming a slanting linear structure at a sharp angle surmounted by a metal *púrnakalasa* at the top. The wooden galleries of the storeys are beautifully carved, each following the same basic pattern. Each slanting roof consists of rows of slates, much like the roofs on the pent-roofed temples, designed to shed water and ice in winters. Following are a few case studies best illustrating the features listed above.

Lakshana Devi Temple

Dedicated to Devi Lakhna, a local name given to the goddess Mahisasuramardini, a form of Durga, it is a seventh-century wooden structure at the southwest corner of the Chaurasi Siddha temple complex in Bharmaur, the series of modifications over the years clearly visible. Most of the structure was made with deodar wood, which currently does not stand out as it does in some other temples of the same period owing to the obvious cleaning, scrubbing, painting and restructuring of the temple. It is constructed in pent-roofed style, with alternate courses of wood and stone covered by a roof with schist tiles. The entrance is through an impressive wooden façade with three sections: an intricately carved doorframe with various cornices, a rectangular portion dividing the doorframe and pediment, and a triangular pediment on top. A typical example of wood carving on temple elements, its study in some detail is required.

The innermost doorjamb is a broad space with a profusion of vegetal patterns in shallow relief emerging from the navels of two couples on the bottom left and bottom right, and ending at the tails of two birds facing each other at the top middle of the jamb, their beaks connected. The second jamb displays a narrow vegetal scroll preceded by a rather complex figural *Sakha*. The bottom-most space is occupied by *yaksA as* each followed by sinuous figures of Ganga and Yamuna with their respective *va hanas*. Full-bodied figures of deities followed the two goddesses: in succession, Surya, Vishnu, Siva above Ganga, a goddess with covered head, Siva, a possible Kartikeya above Yamuna. The lintel portion is occupied by flying male figures, four on each side interspersed with what seem to be garlands of flowers. The third fillet of the doorjamb consists of a worn-down scroll of rosettes meeting at the centre of the lintel on a *ki rtimukha*. A figural scroll comes next, with unidentifiable figures (possibly deities) in high relief one over the other, each in *tribhan ga* posture. Its lintel is most interesting: beautiful figures of Vidyadharas with long hair and holding weapons or musical instruments decorate the fillet in a variety of attitudes. The last jamb is semi-circular in cross-section, a vegetal scroll arising from a pot on each side. A rampant lion facing inwards is depicted at the top of each side, with a rider on its hindquarters.

The rectangular portion directly above the doorframe has three registers. Ten curved niches housing *mithuna* couples in dynamic attitudes are held up by pillared capitals in the lower register. The central register contains 11 dancing female figures separated by panels holding defaced figures, presently unidentifiable. The upper register again displays 10 arched niches with animal-headed squatting figures. The uppermost portion, the triangular pediment, contains a rather weathered figure of a three-headed Vishnu on a personified Garuda, his *va hana*, within a trefoil arch. Lying directly below the framed arch is a rich frieze of cross-legged *navagrahas*.

Another wood-carved element of importance in this temple is the ceiling, in both the *manòdòapa* and the cella. The *manòdòapa* ceiling is divided into five square compartments each accommodating a full-blown lotus with eight petals bordered with bands of scrolls and chequered patterns. The central compartment represents the abovementioned 'lantern' ceiling, with superimposed square elements set obliquely in layers to create a succession. The cella ceiling is much like the *manòdòapa*'s in style and crafting, except that it is rectangular. The triangular spaces between the diagonal rectangles that house the lotus are filled with figures bending on one knee alternating with vegetal patterns. The cella door is wooden as well, ornamented with pot-and-foliage motifs and rosette scrolls. Even the wooden pillars of the *manòdòapa* are similarly decorated, the brackets usually depicting demigods and celestial beings.

Lakshana Devi temple is by far the most interesting and complex study of wooden art and architecture in the Himalayan hills. Sophisticated wood-carving on every element of this classical temple proves the blanket use of wood as a raw material, instead of stone as is the case in other regions. A brief overview of a few other sacred sites of these hills should help illuminate this practice of wood carving more profoundly.

Shakti Devi Temple

Twenty-five kilometres from Bharmaur lies the village of Chhattrari where an old wooden shrine, of the same period as the Lakshana Devi temple, enshrines a brass image of Shakti Devi. The temple consists of a cella with a narrow *manòdòapa* in the front, the pillars and ceiling of which are similar to the Bharmaur shrine in style and ornamentation, but less remarkable. The walls of the temples are now plastered, and covered with mythological paintings, perhaps a later addition of the 18th-19th centuries. The cella doorway with six elaborately carved jambs demands attention. The innermost jambs have *yaksA□as* at the base sprouting creepers that fill up the entire space culminating in the figure of Gajalakshmi at the centre of the lintel. A figural band with Ganga and Yamuna at the base follows a narrow floral scroll. On the lintel 12 multi-armed personages can be identified. The following jamb is cylindrical with vegetal scrolls issuing from the mouth of a *ki□rtimukha* on the lintel. The last one has three standing figures on each side alternating with small *ganòa* figures. A row of flying celestials make up the lintel.

Mrikula Devi Temple

Mrikula Devi temple in Udaipur, Lahaul, dedicated to Kali presents an interesting mix of Brahmanic and Buddhist influences. The exterior of the temple and the image in the sanctum are later additions, probably of the 17th century, but the inside of the shrine is much older (c. 10th century). A few pillars, the sanctum doorway and the *manòdòapa* ceiling may be ascribed to the early period, whereas the window panels and the ceiling architraves were added later or reproduced.

Fig. : Mrikula Devi Temple, Udaipur, Lahaul

The ceiling is divided into nine compartments, the central square depicting a large lotus surrounded by *ki□rtimukha*, *makaras*, and *vajras*, symbolic of Buddhist engagements. Panels around the central compartments depict flying celestial figures with weapons and musical instruments. The panel on the west displays Shiva with his *pariva□ra-devata□s*. On the northern side the panel exhibits not a Brahmanical but a Buddhist theme, that of the Buddha subduing Mara. Dressed in monastic robes, Buddha is shown seated while Mara's army of demons, and his beautiful daughters try to distract him. The latter stage architraves show Vishnu in his Trivikrama incarnation (Vamana in his giant form), complete with each individual deity. The opposite panel displays the myth of the churning of the ocean. From the outside, the shrine presents a juxtaposition of ancient and modern architectural elements. The structure itself very ordinary; the inside is remarkable, a breathtaking overall effect of intense wood-carving, very precise and animated.

Indigenous Wooden Temples

This category of Himalayan temples is ascribed to centuries later than the period of previously discussed classical temples. Wood being the primary raw material for construction, temples were perpetually renewed owing to the loss due to rather frequent forest fires, lightning, and earthquakes. These structures were either made entirely of wood, or a combination of wooden beams and stone blocks, the plan almost equivalent to that of the classical shrines. The distinguishing 'folkish' element of these structures is the extended elevation, successive storeys atop the roof of the main shrine forming a pagoda structure, conical in shape, imitating the northern *na□gara*style of temple building. A few examples of such multi-tiered pyramidal temples are Hidimba Devi temple, Manali; Parashar Rishi temple, Mandi; Mahadeva temple, Kullu; Bhimakali temple, Sarahan; and Bhawani temple, Shimla. The following section brings one such shrine into focus.

Set in the hills of Mandi district, the Parashar Rishi temple is situated on a lakeside harbouring one of the finest examples of wood-carving, meticulously incorporating classical artistic elements in folk. Built by Raja Ban Sen in about 1340 CE, this was originally a shrine for a local *nag devata* turned into a brahmanic temple for Rishi Parashar. Modern architectural influence is evident from the luxurious embellishment on the outer wall of the sanctum. In O.C. Handa's words, 'The first outermost narrow strip carries a deeply undercut elaborately curvilinear scroll running all through on both the ends. This element is succeeded by a wider one on which a complex form of a serpent, with its pulsating and scaly body knotted to form reef knots, is carved in very bold and well-moulded relief. Its tail is dangling over the full bloom lotus in the hand of Vishnu at the bottom. The inner side of these jambs depicts almost freestanding snakes creeping swiftly upward' (Handa 2006:162). Similar serpent depictions are seen on other elements of the temple as well, along with a variety of figural and vegetal motifs. Thus, the tutelary deity of the region, the Naga *devata* still holds predominance over the shrine, exhibited clearly in its ornamentation.

Secular Architecture

Scholars use a local term applied to the indigenous population of Himalayan region, *khash*, in the context of its secular architecture. The residential houses of these *khash* people seem to be bereft of the embellishment on wooden surfaces commonly visible on wooden temples. Even in traditional residences only vacant exposed wooden surfaces are found with a stark absence of ornamental woodwork. The reason could be that the aesthetic and artistic sensibility these people had was entirely committed to religiosity: hence, the intensive wood-carving tradition on hill temples, almost on all the wooden ones. Only a few exceptions remain, two of which are now discussed.

The ancient palace of Guge Rani at Sapani in Kinnaur is one example, where a few pillars and wall panels still remain in their original wooden state with deep-chiselled anthropomorphic and floral carvings. Figural themes in deep relief include various incarnations of and mythical episodes related to Vishnu. The pillars display intensive floral ornamentation, the pot-and-foliage motif being most popular, with leonine figures over *makaras* in brackets. It is believed that this palace could have originally been a temple dedicated to Bhimakali (11th-12th century CE), the deduction a result of the religious themes and figural carving. A few panels of the later period, possibly 17th century, when the structure officially became a residence for the kinnauri princess Guge Rani, depict a 10-armed image of Durga and a

Mahisasuramardini. Another such building is the Kardar Kothi at Bharmaur, ascribed to Raja Prithvi Singh (1641–1664 CE) of Chamba. This structure contains one of the finest figurative woodcarvings, and scholars believe that alongside the work of local Hindu artisans there were Kashmiri influences on the structure, evident in the use of cusped arches and geometrical woodwork.

In one of the panels on the porch of the kothi are depicted the figures of Hanuman, Ram and Sita seated together framed by a cusped arch; in another lie figures of Siva, Brahma and Vishnu in the same style. The door of the kothi itself displays individual carved portraits of the Raja within a cusped-arch frame. These overlapping influences seem to be essential in framing a development of architectural, particularly secular, traits over the centuries.

Other architectural features of residential buildings in the hills include the very specific technique of building walls in wood and stone. Here, wooden planks are placed on edges with a slight gap between them.

Over these similar planks are placed, but this time placed across. This process is repeated to form a vertical arrangement of wooden planks with uniform gaps in between. These are then filled with hand-packed stones or stone chips. The sides are then finished with plaster. Modern structures often incorporate the use of brick instead of stone. The wooden binders tie the whole structure together providing them gravitational stability, they can withstand lateral pressures for years. This technique improved over the years with better stone quality; mica-schist came to be used later, and perfected as the kath-khuni technique. These wooden beams and stone walls attained different nomenclatures in different regions of the hills: *doriya* in Kinnaur, *cheol* in Shimla, and *patari* in Mandi and Kullu. To economise on the use of wood, often more than one course of stone is used per wooden beam, so the building from the outside looks like a stone structure with a few wooden beams spaced apart.

Wooden Sculptures

It was earlier discussed that the region of Himachal Pradesh worshipped cultic deities, tutelary gods, often demonic and wrathful in nature. Human beings, at some point, must have needed an image of some kind to communicate with such forces and to pacify through proper propitiation.

Fig. : Wooden Masks, Shakti Devi Temple, Chhattrari

It is not entirely impossible that the earliest images representing such entities placed in dense forests could have come from the forests itself. A reproduction of facial features to give some sort of a form to a wooden piece seems plausible. Hence, the earliest woodcarving produced could have been a facial image, symbolic representations of invisible primitive demonic deities, or what we now know as masks. The modern metallic masks of gods and goddesses so popular in Himalayan regions could be successors of wooden *mohras*. In course of time these objects were taken from their dwelling and ushered into the community on special occasions, where the priest of the deity could wear such a *mohra* to hide his real face behind it, 'masking' his true identity. With time, these masks, besides representing demonic forces, also came to be used in theatrical performances, for religious purposes and entertainment. Currently, their primary function is to serve as *devatâs*, or local deities, at the popular fairs of the hills, like Úivarâtri in Mandi and Kullu Dussehrâ, where they are affixed on palanquins, or hung on temple walls. These exist in groups, a group or more ascribed to a particular shrine, a shrine or more belonging to a particular village. Several wooden masks presently belong with the Shimla state museum. A few such 'demon' masks lie in the sanctuary of Shakti Devi temple at Chhattrari, where they are worn by villagers who enact an annual ritual between the devi and evil spirts.

From the village of Gajan in Kullu district come six wooden sculptures preserved in the temple complex of the twin goddesses Docha-Mocha. Two male images, possibly cultic, and four female images, fulfilling an architectural function have been preserved at this site. The male deity figure, carved in the round, is now much weathered, but some characteristic features nevertheless can be made out. The presence of a halo indicates its divinity, ornamentation, dress (long tunic and waistband) and a crown of a specific type give the impression of it being a Surya image. The second male deity is even more damaged than the previous one, all that remains being the lower garment resembling the animal skin typically worn by ascetics. The four female figures are in all probability *yaksA□i* images, also called *vrikshika*s or *shalabhanjika*s in this context, as they stand under flowering trees, with sinuous bodies and ornamented attire, a popular temple motif.

Thus, we see a gradual development of wooden art and architectural practices, from the making of simple masks to sculpting divinities, embellishing temple elements with complex wood carving, and applying constructive techniques to built structures: a juxtaposition of classical and indigenous traditions that creates unique trends in the artistic practices of Himachal.

10

Education

EDUCATION IN HIMACHAL PRADESH

Himachal Pradesh was under the direct control of the British colonial rule in the mid 19th century. Also, the state was the summer capital of India during the British colonial rule. Hence, the standard of education provided in the state has reached to a considerably high level. The state has several highly reputed educational institutions for higher studies.

The Indian Institute of Technology Mandi, Himachal Pradesh University (HPU) and the National Institute of Technology(NIT), NIT Hamirpur are some of the pioneer institutions located in the state. The University Grants Commission (UGC) has allocated Rs 45 million to Himachal Pradesh University in the 10th plan which is an increase of nearly 70% over the ninth one. Dr. Yashwant Singh Parmar University of Horticulture and Forestry has gained a unique distinction not only in the nation but also in whole of Asia for imparting teaching, research and extension education in horticulture, forestry and allied disciplines.

The government is working constantly to prepare various plans to strengthen the education system of Himachal. The state government has decided to start up with 3 major nursing colleges to develop the health system in the state.

Himachal has one of the highest literacy rates in India. Hamirpur District is among the top districts in the country for literacy. Education rates among women are quite encouraging in the state.

Himachal Pradesh is home to many educational institutions offering a wide variety of courses. There are five universities, two medical colleges, four dental colleges and two engineering colleges in the state. There are over 10,000 primary schools, 1,000 secondary schools and more than 1,300 high schools in Himachal. Hindi and English are compulsory languages in schools whereas Punjabi, Sanskrit, Tamil, Telugu and Urdu are chosen as optional languages.

In meeting the constitutional obligation to make primary education compulsory, Himachal has now became the first state in India to make elementary education accessible to every child in the state. Himachal Pradesh government is also very keen to transform this state into an education hub. In March 2008, Government of India made an announcement stating that as part of the 11th five-year plan, an Indian Institute of Technology will be established in this state. Further, Atal Bihari Vajpayee Government Engineering and Technology Institute has been started at Pragatinagar, in Shimla district. This college will have engineering related courses such as ITI, Diploma and Degree all in same campus.

Indira Gandhi Medical College and Hospital at Shimla

At the time of Independence, Himachal Pradesh had a literacy rate of 8% - one of the lowest in the country. By 2011, the literacy rate surged to over 82%, making Himachal one of the most literate states in the country. There are over 10,000 primary schools, 1,000 secondary schools and more than 1,300 high schools in the state. In meeting the constitutional obligation to make primary education compulsory, Himachal became the first state in India to make elementary education accessible to every child. Although gender bias in education levels is a prominent issue all over India, Himachal Pradesh is one of the exceptions. The state has a female literacy rate of around 76%. In addition, school enrollment and participation rates for girls are almost universal at the primary level. While higher levels of education do reflect a gender based disparity, Himachal is still significantly ahead of other states at bridging the gap. The HamirpurDistrict in particular stands out for high literacy rates across all metrics of measurement.

Indian Institute of Advanced Study at Shimla

The state government has played an instrumental role in the rise of literacy in the state by spending a significant proportion of the state's GDP on education. During the first six five-year plans, most of the development expenditure in education sector was utilized in quantitative expansion, but after the seventh five-year-plan the state government switched emphasis on qualitative improvement and modernisation of education. In an effort to raise the number of teaching staff at primary schools they appointed over 1000 teacher aids through the Vidya Upasak Yojna in 2001. The Sarva Shiksha Abhiyan is another HP government initiative that not only aims for universal elementary education but also encourages communities to engage in the management of schools. The Rashtriya Madhayamic Shiksha Abhiyan launched in 2009, is a similar scheme but focuses on improving access to quality secondary education.

The standard of education in the state has reached a considerably high level as compared to other states in India with several reputed educational institutes for higher studies. The Indian Institute of Technology Mandi, Indian Institute of Management Sirmaur, Himachal Pradesh University in Shimla, National Institute of Technology, Hamirpur, Indian Institute of Information Technology Una, Alakh Prakash Goyal University and Baddi University of Emerging Sciences and Technologies are some of the notable universities in the state.

Indira Gandhi Medical College and Hospital in Shimla, Dr. Rajendra Prasad Government Medical College in Kangra, Rajiv Gandhi Government Post Graduate Ayurvedic College in Paprola and Homoeopathic Medical College & Hospital in Kumarhatti are the prominent medical institutes in the state. Besides these, there is a Government Dental College in Shimla which is the state's first recognised dental institute.

The state government has also decided to start three major nursing colleges to develop the healthcare system of the state. CSK Himachal Pradesh Krishi Vishwavidyalya Palampur is one of the most renowned hill agriculture institutes in the world. Dr. Yashwant Singh Parmar University of Horticulture and Forestry has earned a unique distinction in India for imparting teaching, research and extension education in horticulture, forestry and allied disciplines.

Further, state-run Jawaharlal Nehru Government Engineering College was inaugurated in 2006 at Sundernagar. Himachal Pradesh also hosts a campus of the prestigious fashion college, National Institute of Fashion Technology (NIFT) in Kangra.

EDUCATIONAL INSTITUTES

- Alakh Prakash Goyal University
- Dr. Yashwant Singh Parmar University of Horticulture and Forestry
- Green Hills Engineering College
- Himachal University
- IITT college of Engineering
- Indian Institute of Advanced Study
- Institute of Engineering and Emerging Technologies
- National Institute of Technology, Hamirpur
- Jaypee University of Information Technology
- Chitkara University, Himachal Pradesh
- Lawrence School
- University Institute of Information Technology (UIIT)

ENGINEERING INSTITUTIONS

National Institute of Technology, Hamirpur, (Admin block)

The state of Himachal Pradesh is a late starter in establishing engineering institutes as compared to other states of India. National

Institute of Technology, Hamirpur (then *Regional Engineering College, Hamirpur*) was the first institute established in 1986. IITT college of Engineering, Kala Amb was the second institute established in the 20th century. The remaining institutes were established in the 21st century. A Government engineering school namely, Jawaharlal Nehru Government Engineering College in Sundernagar, was established by state govt in 2006. Needless to say that none of these institutions have achieved academic maturity as yet. Though some institutions (notably National Institute of Technology, Hamirpur) are striving hard to be centrs of excellence, however the results are not encouraging. People of Himachal Pradesh nurture a desire to make this state a Switzerland of India because both share similar topography, however Himachal Pradesh lacks Swiss industrial prowess at present. It is hoped that manpower trained at these institutions shall support the industries in the region and some budding entrepreneurs will emerge to transform the industrial landscape of the state.

Educational institutions (non-governmental)

Himachal Pradesh is home to several non-governmental organisations (NGO) operating educational institutes in the state.

- Deer Park Institute offers educational courses and seminars in classical Indian wisdom traditions.
- Dharmalaya Institute provides education and vocational training in vernacular earthen architecture in the traditional Kangra style, as well as service-learning courses in sustainable living and immersive ecotourism programs.
- NISHTHA is a charitable trust working for the benefit and development of society as a whole by improving the welfare of families with particular focus on women and children, through activities in the fields of health, education and environment.
- Shantideva Homeopathic Research Institute (SHRI) runs educational programs to increase awareness of healthy lifestyles, offering free clinics and seminars for the rural population of Himachal Pradesh.

Dr Puran Chand Medical Charitable Trust (Regd) runs a number of Institutions in the State – Himachal Dental College, Sundernagar (District Mandi), Himachal Institute of Dental Sciences, Himachal Institute of Technology, Himachal Institute of Nursing, Himachal Institute of Life Sciences, and Himachal Institute of Pharmacy all at Paonta Sahib (District Sirmaur)

UNIVERSITIES AND COLLEGES

Dr. Yashwant Singh Parmar University of Horticulture and Forestry

Dr. Yashwant Singh Parmar University of Horticulture and Forestry in district Solan, Himachal Pradesh, India is the first University of its kind in Asia with an exclusive mandate of education, research and extension in Horticulture and Forestry.

People usually use the short form of the university name : Dr. Y S Parmar University of Horticulture and Forestry.

It covers 5.5 km^2 and is situated in Nauni on the Solan-Rajgarh Road. The campus lies 15 km from the town of Solan. The University was established on December 1, 1985 and is named after the first Chief Minister of Himachal Pradesh.

This University was inaugurated by the Late Rajiv Gandhi, Prime Minister of India, on 30 April 1988.

It has two colleges, namely, the College of Horticulture and the College of Forestry, which are sub-divided into 14 departments and are looked after by a faculty of over 200 scientists and teachers.

It also has a school specialized in the study of apples, called Apple School, Nauni.

It offers under-graduate, post-graduate and doctoral courses in horticulture, forestry and allied disciplines.

Green Hills Engineering College

Objectives

- The computer centre aims to create a computing environment for the search of academic management.
- To endow professional services to students, staff and administration.
- To endorse and assist the use of advance computing technology.

Infrastructure

At present the computer centre is housed in the administrative block. The center has well equipped machinery (Xn Servers and P-IV machines). Nearly, 100 nodes are accessible with heterogeneous Intranet over the Windowing, Unix and Netware environments. Centre has endorsed 128kbps link providing Internet facility to the users (*centre*).

Achievements

- A State of the Art Local Area Network.
- 60 networked clients with email and web browsing facilities.
- Numerous Network Servers and Desktop computers and Printers already networked.
- Internet facilities available to all
- Hardware/Software and Installation Support facilities.

Library

All students and staff of *Green Hills Engineering College* needs to be the member of the library. Facilities provide to the members:

- Lending
- Photostat
- CDROM collection
- Reference section

- Audio visual
- Book bank

Library is having a total collection of 5771 books.

The Workshop

The Central Workshop was started in 2003 to impart training to the undergraduate students. The Central Workshop is well equipped with advanced machinery. The various sections of the workshop includes:

- Machine Shop
- Welding Shop
- Carpentry Shop
- Sheet Metal Shop
- Fitting Shop
- Electrical Shop
- Black smithy Shop
- Foundry and Moulding Shop
- Automobile Repairing Shop.

HIMACHAL UNIVERSITY

Type	Public university
Chancellor	V. S. Kokje
Vice-Chancellor	Professor L. R. Verma
Chief Minister	Virbhadra Singh
Location	Shimla, India

Himachal Pradesh University is a public university in Shimla, India.

Departments

- Department of Bio-Sciences
- Department of Bio-Technology
- Department of Buddhist Studies (Bhoti Language)
- Department of Chemistry
- Department of Computer Science

- Department of Commerce
- Department of English
- Department of Economics
- Department of Education
- Department of Geography
- Department of Hindi
- Department of History
- Institute of Management Studies (IMS)
- Institute of Vocational Studies (MTA)
- Department of Journalism and Mass Communication
- Department of Laws
- Department of Modern European and Foreign Languages
- Department of Mathematics
- Department of Performing Arts
- Department of Physics
- Department of Physical Education
- Department of Political Science
- Department of Psychology
- Department of Public Administration
- Department of Sanskrit
- Department of Sociology
- Department of Visual Arts
- Department of Yoga Studies
- University Institute of Information Technology

In order to impart training to students in the state-of-the-art Information Technology, the Executive Council of the University in its meetings held on 4th March, 2000 and 29th June, 2000 decided to start a five year integrated Master Course in Information Technology namely MIT/BIT.

The purpose has been to produce professional leaders in the field of Information Technology, as also to enhance technological strength of the region and the country.

To run this course with model curriculum, the University Institute of Information Technology (UIIT) was set up with the latest IT infrastructure and an experienced faculty. As per the University Grants Commission (UGC), New Delhi directions, the nomenclature of the course was changed to Master of Technology in Information Technology M.Tech.(IT)/ Bachelor of Technology in Information Technology B. Tech. (IT).

As per the list of specified degrees by University Grants commission, New Delhi. From the year 2003-2004 the B.Tech in Information Technology programme has been approved by the All India Council of Technical Education, New Delhi, bringing the course in the main stream of Technical Education.

NOTABLE ALUMNI

- 1983: Hamid Karzai, Masters in International Relations & Political Science
- 2003: Hamid Karzai, President of Afghanistan, Honorary degree of Doctor of Literature from Dr. Suraj Bhan, Chancellor
- 2003: Tsering Dundup-(Public Relation Officer, Tibetan youth congress, 2004) master's degree in Geography, Gold Medallist

INDIAN INSTITUTE OF ADVANCED STUDY

Established	1965
Type	Research Institution
Location	Shimla, Himachal Pradesh India

The Indian Institute of Advanced Study is a prestigious research institute based in Shimla, India. It was set up by the Ministry of Education, Government of India in 1964 and it started functioning from October 20, 1965.

History and Establishment

The building that houses the Institute was originally built as a home for Lord Dufferin, Viceroy of India from 1884-1888 and was called the Viceregal Lodge. It housed all the subsequent viceroys and governor generals of India. It occupied the Observatory Hill, one of the seven hills that Shimla is built upon.

The building was designed by Henry Irvine, an architect in the Public Works Department at that time. The Viceregal Lodge had electricity as far back as 1888, much before the rest of the town of Shimla.

Many historic decisons have been taken in the building during the Indian independence movement. The Shimla Conference was held here in 1945. The decision to carve out Pakistan and East Pakistan from India was also taken here in 1947.

After India gained independence, the building was renamed Rashtrapati Niwas and was used as a summer retreat for the President of India. However, due to its neglect, Dr. S Radhakrishnan decided to turn it into a centre of higher learning.

The Indian Institute of Advanced Study was first created as a society on 6 October 1964. The institute was formally inaugurated by Prof. S. Radhakrishnan on 20 October 1965.

Around 2004, a rare Stické court was discovered on the grounds of the Viceregal Lodge complex.

Administration

The Institute is administered by a Society and a Governing Body, the members of which come from varied backgrounds. A statutory Finance Committee advises the Governing body in financial matters.

The Director of the Institute is assisted by a Secretary, a Deputy Secretary a Public Relations Officer and other supervisory staff.

Academics

The fellows of the Institute currently focus on the following areas:

- Humanities
    - Arts and Aesthetics

   - Comparative Study of Literature
   - Study of Religion and Philosophy.
- Social Sciences
   - Development Studies
   - Comparative Study of Political Institutions
   - Socioeconomic and Socio-Cultural Formation in Historical Perspective.
- Natural and Life Sciences
   - State Policies on Science and Technology
   - Science, Technology and Development
   - Methodologies and Techniques.

Alumni

Burmese Nobel Laureate Aung San Suu Kyi was a fellow of the Institute from February 1987 to February 1989.

NATIONAL INSTITUTE OF TECHNOLOGY, HAMIRPUR

Established	1986
Type	Deemed University
Director	I. K. Bhat
Location	Hamirpur, Himachal Pradesh, India
Campus	200 acres

National Institute of Technology, Hamirpur or NIT Hamirpur is a national level university, of India, imparting undergraduate and postgraduate level education in engineering and architecture. The institute also runs its own doctorate programmes.

History

Established in 1986 as Regional Engineering College, Hamirpur in Hamirpur district of Himachal Pradesh, it was a joint enterprise of the Government of India and the Government of Himachal Pradesh.

Come 26th June, 2002 REC Hamirpur was awarded the status of deemed-to-be university and upgraded into a NIT. As a result of this transition the institute came under the sole purview of the Government of India.

The Institute

NIT Hamirpur currently has 7 academic departments, namely:

- Applied Sciences & Humanities
- Architecture
- Civil Engineering
- Computer Science & Engineering
- Electrical Engineering
- Electronics & Communication Engineering
- Mechanical Engineering

Students are admitted through their performance in the All-India Engineering Entrance Examination (AIEEE), held every year. The academic year starts from early August and terminates in late May.

The semester system of education is followed and each academic year consists of an odd and an even semester, which are punctuated by a short winter vacation during late December and early January, and a longer summer vacation spanning June and July.

Engineering undergraduates need to successfully complete eight semesters in order to be awarded Bachelor of Technology, while their counterparts in the field of architecture need to complete ten semesters to be awarded Bachelor of Architecture. The post-graduate runs for a duration of four semesters and a degree of Master of Technology is awarded.

In 2006 PhD programmes were started in different departments.

COMPUTER SCIENCE AND ENGINEERING

Department of Computer Science & Engineering was established in the year 1989 with the initial intake of 15 students which was subsequently increased to 30 in 1995. The department has got its own building with an effective area of 1942 sqm. The Computer Centre is also housed in the department building.

The new building for the Institute Computer Centre is under construction.

The Institute has dedicated 2 Mbps leased line and 512 Kbps VSAT link for Internet connectivity. The Internet facility is available round the clock in the academic area and the same facility has been extended upto 1500 nodes in the hostels and residences throughout the campus with integrated VoIP phone facility.

The intake was increased to 45 in the year 2005 and from year 2006 onwards it was further increased to 60 students.

The present infrastructure is excellent to carry out research and other academic work by UG and PG students.

The department is equipped with various high end Servers (Sun ultra SPARC-III), Graphics Workstations (Silicon Graphics and Intel P-IV 3.4 GHz with 1 GB RAM), P-IV machines, Laptop, Scanners, Laser Printers etc.

The placements of Final Year students is 100% and around 50% of students in 3rd year are placed in reputed organizations.

ELECTRICAL ENGINEERING

The Department of Mechanical Engineering came into its existence right from the inception of the then Regional Engineering College Hamirpur (now National Institute of Technology Hamirpur) in the year 1986 and served as catering department to other disciplines.

The discipline of Mechanical Engineering started offering undergraduate programme leading to four year Bachelor of Technology (B.Tech) degree in Mechanical Engineering in the year 1994.

The first batch was started with an intake of 30 students which has now been enhanced to 60 students by the Ministry of HRD, Government of India from the session 2006-2007.

MECHANICAL ENGINEERING

The Board of Governors and the Senate are the two main administrative bodies of the institute. Administrative decisions regarding academics are taken by a committee comprising of:

- Dr. I.K. Bhat, Director
- Dr. R.L. Sharma, Dean (P&D)
- Dr. Rakesh Sehgal, Dean (IR&C)
- Dr. A.S. Singha, Dean (Academics & International Programmes)
- Dr. Anoop Kumar, Dean (Students & Alumni Affairs)
- Sh. G.R. Bharti, Registrar
- Er. Vinod Kapoor, Training & Placement Officer
- Er. P.K. Sood, Workshop Superintendent
- Sh. D.S. Jaswal, Senior Librarian
- Dr. Y.D. Sharma, Chief Warden
- Sh. R.K. Jamalta, Sports Officer
- Dr. Piar Chand, NCC Officer

The current members of the Board of Governors are:

- Dr. R.L. Chauhan, Chairman
- Sh. Ravi Mathur
- Sh. P. Mitra
- Sh. S.M. Bhardwaj
- Dr. Surendra Prasad
- Dr. D. Swaminadhan
- Dr. K. Madhu Murthy
- Er. Ramanand Sharma
- Sh. J.P. Gaur
- Sh. Sachit Jain
- Dr. V.K. Sarda
- Dr. Lalit K. Awasthi
- Dr. I.K. Bhat
- Financial Advisor (HRD), Government of India, Ministry of Human Resources & Development

The Senate is chaired by the Director.

Campus Life

The institute campus is situated in Anu in Hamirpur district of Himachal Pradesh, India. The campus is at an altitude of 900 metres above sea level and overlooks the Dhauladhar range. It is approximately 4 kilometres from the main bus terminus of Hamirpur town on the National Highway running through Hamirpur and Toni Devi. Being a residential institute, there are five boys' hostels and one girls' hostels in the campus along with separate residences for the faculty and staff. Each hostel has its own peculiarities. Some have four-seated or triple-seated rooms, while others have doublets and singlets. The different hostels are:

- Dhauladhar Boys' Hostel
- Kailash Boys' Hostel
- Manimahesh Boys' Hostel
- Parvati Girls' Hostel
- Shivalik Boys' Hostel
- Vindhyachal Boys' Hostel

The canteen, juice bar, Nescafe coffee bar and the nearby Ekta Cafe are some of the most frequented jaunts. Not to forget Tilak's Dhaba, which serves delicious dishes even in the middle of the night when the examinations are in full swing. The complete absence of a movie hall in the district is overcome by the fortnighly movie shows held in the auditorium.

Hill 'Ffair and Nimbus are the official cultural and technical festivals respectively. Nimbus is a comparatively younger event than Hill 'Ffair. During the days of Hill 'Ffair the open air theatre becomes the nerve-centre for all activity. The rock show, fashion parade, and the Mr. & Miss Hill 'Ffair competitions are some of the most popular events. Mr. Sanchit Gupta and Miss Mansi Dulloo are the current holders of the Mr. & Miss Hill 'Ffair titles.

A number of extracurricular activities are organized throughout the year by the ISTE students chapter of NIT

Hamirpur. The newly formed GNU/Linux User Group of NIT Hamirpur organizes workshops, demonstrations, presentations all throughout the year. The students are also running a literacy mission to help the poor children residing in and around the campus to stay ahead in life. Art of Living sessions are also organized regularly at subsidized rates for those residing in the campus.

LAWRENCE SCHOOL, SANAWAR

Sanawar Logo	*Never Give In*
Foundation	15 April 1847
School type	Public School
Head Master	Mr. Praveen Vashisht
Chairman of Trustees	Secretary of Education, Government of India
Location	Kasauli Hills, Himachal Pradesh
Pupils	700
Teaching Staff	70
Houses	Himalaya, Nilagiri, Siwalik, Vindhya

The Lawrence School, Sanawar (near Kasauli), Himachal Pradesh, India was founded by Major General Sir Henry Montgomery Lawrence of the Army of the colonial India's British Raj as a military asylum. It was established on 15 April 1847, and is one of the oldest coeducational boarding schools in the world.

The school has graduated many dignitaries and is a reputed coeducational, residential public school of India.

The Background: Henry Lawrence wanted to establish a chain of schools with a view to provide education to the children of the deceased and serving soldiers and officers of the British army. Lawrence was himself killed in the Indian rebellion of 1857, also called India's First War of Independence. His dream took shape and four such schools, initially known as Lawrence Military Asylum, were established in different parts of India: the first two during his lifetime in the year 1847 at Sanawar and the second at Mount Abu in 1856; the third at Lovedale, near Ootacamund on 6 September 1858, and the fourth in Ghora Gali (near Murree, now in Pakistan) in 1860.

History: Founded by Sir Henry and Lady Honoria Lawrence, Sanawar is believed to be the first coeducational boarding school in the world. On 15 April 1847, a group of 14 boys and girls camped at the top of the foothills of the Himalayas. They lived under canvas for some weeks anxiously waiting for the first buildings to be completed before the arrival of the monsoon. Thus did Sanawar come into existence.

By 1853, the school had grown to 195 pupils when it was presented with the King's Colour. One of only six schools and colleges ever to be so honoured in the entire British Empire, the others being Eton, Shrewsbury, Cheltenham, the Duke of York's Royal Military School and the Royal Military College, Sandhurst, Sanawar has held its Colour for the longest unbroken period.

From its Foundation, the financial burden of the School was borne by Sir Henry until his death in 1857, when the government assumed responsibility for the finances as a mark of esteem to his memory. Under these arrangements, control of the School passed from the 'Honourable Board of Directors' to the Crown. This was a most unusual arrangement, not repeated in any English Public School.

The tradition of military training at Sanawar has always been strong and was of such a high standard that several contingents of boys were enlisted from the School and sent straight to the battlefields of the Great War. In appreciation of this, the School was redesignated in 1920 as the "Lawrence Royal Military School", and, in 1922, the Prince of Wales personally presented the School with new Colours. The School Colour continues to this day to be trooped at the Founders Celebration in early October and Sanawar pupils continue to make a major contribution to the defence of the country to this day, most notably in the form of Arun Khetarpal, a Param Vir Chakra awardee.

Sanawar's Centenary year (1947) was crucial to the development of the School. With Independence, the bulk of the staff and children at Sanawar returned to the UK. However, the then Governor General, Lord Louis Mountbatten, presided at the School's Centenary celebrations and read out a special message from George VI. Thereafter, control of the School passed from the Crown to the Government of India, Ministry of Defence. A further transfer in 1949 brought the School under the control of the Ministry of Education and subsequently, in 1953, to the autonomous Lawrence School (Sanawar) Society. However, Sanawar retains strong links with its past. The Chairman of the Society is the Secretary for Education, Government of India and, at the recent sesquicentenary celebrations in 1997, a message of congratulations was received from the current Prince of Wales, Prince Charles.

The first Principal of the School was the Rev. W. J. Parker, (1848-1863). Notable events during his period include the first Founder's Day in 1849, and the opening of the Chapel in 1851. Parker was followed by the Rev. J. Cole (1864-1886), the Rev. A. Hilldersley (1886-1912) and by the fourth Principal, the Rev. G. D. Barne (1912-1932) who developed Sanawar into a major public school along English lines with House and Prefectorial systems, games on an organised basis and a curriculum working towards Cambridge University Examinations.

The School continued to evolve and modernise throughout the middle and later years of the last century. In 1956, Mr. E. G. Carter, retired as Principal and was succeeded by Major R. Som Dutt (1956-1970), the School's first Indian Headmaster. He laid the foundations for the school, as it is today, India's foremost residential coeducational public school. Developments have continued since that time, most notably under the leadership of Mr. S. R. Das (1974-1988).

Campus: Sanawar is situated on an independent hill and covers an area of 139 acres. The campus is heavily forested with pine, deodar and other conifer trees. To get to the School, one must take a detour from Dharampur on the NH22. Walking around the campus, one can see a mixture of colonial buildings, many of which are over a century old, nestling side by side with modern facilities.

Amongst the oldest buildings is the 140 years old School Chapel with its exquisite stained glass windows. Whilst the school has no specific religious affiliation, the Chapel is the spiritual centre of the community, and regular assemblies are held in which all students and staff take part. The daily routine includes a silent march past the War Memorials beside the Chapel, connecting the pupils of today with those of the past who have played their part in the nations call.

Amongst the new buildings is the Central Dining Hall. The School is constantly upgrading its facilities; most recently, Parker Hall, now the schools' Learning Resource Centre, provides easy access to archival memorabilia, up-to-date library resources, and computer & internet facilities. In this building alone, over thirty new computers have been installed along with the first ISDN line in Himachal Pradesh.

The School takes pride in its state-of-art solar-heated indoor swimming pool, above which is the Indoor Sports Complex and besides which are the squash courts.

Gaskell Hall, named after William Gaskell, used to be the boys school and is now the school Gymnasium. Inter-house Boxing and Gym competition are some of the main events held in Gaskell Hall. On one of the walls of the gymnasium is a quotation from Rudyard Kipling's "Kim", and it reads "Send him to Sanawar and make a man of him."

There are many other buildings and facilities of interest, supporting both academic and non-academic activities. Particularly worthy of mention is the main teaching block, the 'Birdwood School Buildings', which also contains the Barne Hall, where plays, shows, films and lectures are regularly held. Around the school estate are numerous playing fields, the newest being a superb basketball court. The main cricket and football ground, Barnes Field, to which the descent and ascent alone will exhaust, leaves the fittest of players and spectators breathless!

The School is financially self-sufficient and has its own printing press. A resident doctor heads the staff of the Schools 60 bed infirmary, having its own ambulance.

Academics: There are 75 members on the teaching faculty and at the +2 level the subjects offered include English Literature, Computers, Physics, Chemistry, Biology, Psychology, Home Science, Mathematics, Political Science, History, Geography, Hindi, Economics, Commerce, Accountancy, Art, Music and Sculpture.

The ratio of 75 faculty members to about 670 students is far above the average in India.

The normal student strength per classroom varies from 10 to 25.

The school is affiliated to the Central Board of Secondary Education, New Delhi.

There is a growing emphasis on the audio-visual aids in education at Sanawar.

A monthly assessment, in which each student is discussed individually, forms a unique feature of the assessment system at Sanawar.

Very bright students are encouraged with monthly awards of Distinction and Commendation and the privilege of signing the Honours Book once a year. Weak students are placed on the House Masters/Headmasters List and are helped to do remedial work in their weak subjects. A copy of the Assessment Card is sent to the parents. At the end of each term a statement of marks and comments by the subject teachers are also sent to the parents.

The school has an up-to-date library with a substantial collection of books and periodicals on a wide variety, accumulated over the years.

The school museum is not just a collection of articles but an educational experience in much wider sense.

Extra Curricular Activities: Children at Sanawar select a number of 'hobby' activities, which they pursue at different times of the year.

These activities include, for instance:

- Weaving
- Art
- Sculpture
- Ceramics
- Carpentry
- Computers
- Needle Work
- Photography
- Paper Recycling
- Indian Classical Music & Dance
- Bugle and Brass Bands

Also, in line are:

- European Culture Studies
- Western Classical Music

At certain times of the year, children are involved in a wide variety of social activities ranging from fire fighting to working in the School's Rural Centre. Tree planting has been an annual activity over the decades. Other major projects are Adult & Child Education, a Crafts Centre, and annual international village development camps (organized for the Round Square International Service).

Membership of the Round Square International Service gives XIth Class children an opportunity to take part in a student exchange programme with other member schools throughout the world. During a visit of 2 months duration, they study at the host school, staying either with families or in the school's dormitory facilities, playing a full part in the life of the school and community which they are visiting.

Bibliography

Basham, A.L.: *A Cultural History of India*, Oxford, Clarendon Press, 1975.

Desai, Mahadev : *Gandhi and Indian Villages*, New Delhi, Mohit Pub., 2002.

Frauwallner, E..: *History of Indian Philosophy*, Motilal, Delhi, 1973.

Grisenold, H.D.: *Insights into Modern Hinduism*, Oxford, New York, 1934.

Handa, O.C. 2005. *Gaddi Land in Chamba: Its History, Art and Culture*. Chamba: Indus Publishing Company.

Hussein, Abdullah : *Downfall by Degrees*, New Delhi, Katha, 2004.

Ira Mervin Lapidus, *Muslim Cities in the Later Middle Ages*, Cambridge, Mass, 1967.

Krishna Rao M. V.; *Studies in Kautilya*, Munshiram Manoharlal, Delhi, 1979.

Levinson, D.: *Family Violence in Cross Cultural Perspective*, Newbury Park, Sage, 1989.

Macdonell, Arthur A: *Vedic Index of Names and Subjects*. London: Murray, 1912.

Maheshwari, Shriram: *Rural Development in India: A Public Policy Approach*, New Delhi, Sage, 1995.

Mayer, A.: *Caste in an Indian Village: Change and Continuity 1954-1992*, Delhi, OUP, 1996.

Neale, Walter C.: *Economic Change in Rural India: Land Tenure and Reform in the United Provinces, 1800-1955*, New Haven, 1962.

Pal, Adesh, Anupam Nagar and Tapas Chakraborty : *Decolonisation : A Search for Alternatives*, New Delhi, Creative, 2001.

Parel , J.: *Hind Swaraj or Indian Home Rule*, Cambridge University Press, 1925.

Possehl, Gregory L.: *The Harappan Civilization*, London, Aris and Phillips, 1982.

Postel, M. 1985. *Antiquities of Himachal.* Bombay.

Prahlad K.: *Governance and Public Administration for Poverty Reduction*, Salvador, Brazil, 1997.

Prasad, Lal Bahadur : *Indian Political System and Law*, New Delhi, Shree, 2005.

Prithwis Chandra : *Descriptive Bi-Lingual Catalogue of Chinese Books : In the Collection of the Asiatic Society*, Calcutta, Calcutta, Asiatic Society, 2000.

Richard Davis: *Lives of Indian Images,* Princeton Univ. Press. Princeton, 1997.

Richards, J. F. : *The Mughal Empire*, New York: Cambridge University Press, 1993.

Rosenblum, G.: *Law as a Political Instrument,* New York, Random House, 1955.

Roy, Pabitrakumar : *Rabindranath Tagore,* New Delhi, Munshiram Manoharlal, 2002.

Sardesai, Rajdeep: *2014: The Election That Changed India,* Delhi, 2014.

Schwartz, Cowan, Ruth: *A Social History of American Technology.* New York: Oxford University Press, 1996.

Seyla Benhabib: *The Reluctant Modernism of Hannah Arendt*, Rowan and Littlefield Publishers, 2003.

Shani, G.: *Communalism, Caste and Hindu Nationalism: The Violence in Gujarat*, Cambridge Univ Press, Delhi, 2003.

Talageri, Shrikant : *Aryan Invasion Theory and Indian Nationalism,* Voice of India, Delhi, 1993.

Wilbur L.Cross : *The Development of the English Novel*, New Delhi, Atlantic, 2001.

Yadav, Kripal Chandra : *India's Unequal Citizens : A Study of Other Backward Classes,* Manohar, New Delhi, 1994.

Yasin, Mohammad : *Indian Politics : Processes, Issues and Trends,* New Delhi, Kanishka, 2004.

Zaidi, A. Moin: *Evolution of Muslim Political Thought in India,* New Delhi: S. Chand, 1975.

Index

N

P

R

S

T

W

❑❑❑

www.ingramcontent.com/pod-product-compliance
Ingram Content Group UK Ltd.
Pitfield, Milton Keynes, MK11 3LW, UK
UKHW042016290726
14061UKWH00001BB/30